ONE NATION
UNDER GRAHAM

ONE NATION UNDER GRAHAM

Apocalyptic Rhetoric and American Exceptionalism

Jonathan D. Redding

BAYLOR UNIVERSITY PRESS

© 2021 by Baylor University Press
Waco, Texas 76798

Book design by Kasey McBeath
Cover design by *the*BookDesigners
Cover art: Shutterstock/Anthony Correia

Library of Congress Cataloging-in-Publication Data

Names: Redding, Jonathan D., 1987- author.
Title: One nation under Graham : apocalyptic rhetoric and American
    exceptionalism / Jonathan D. Redding.
Description: Waco : Baylor University Press, 2021. | Includes
    bibliographical references and index. | Summary: "Examines the influence
    of Billy Graham's interpretations of Daniel and Revelation in connection
    with the inclusion of "under God" in the USA's Pledge of Allegiance, a
    move that continues to affect contemporary laws and legislation"--
    Provided by publisher.
Identifiers: LCCN 2021015495 (print) | LCCN 2021015496 (ebook) | ISBN
    9781481315197 (hardcover) | ISBN 9781481315807 (pdf) | ISBN
    9781481315210 (epub)
Subjects: LCSH: Graham, Billy, 1918-2018--Influence. | Bellamy, Francis.
    Pledge of Allegience to the Flag. | Christianity and politics. | United
    States--Religion. | Apocalyptic literature.
Classification: LCC BV3785.G69 R43 2021 (print) | LCC BV3785.G69 (ebook)
    | DDC 269.2--dc23
LC record available at https://lccn.loc.gov/2021015495
LC ebook record available at https://lccn.loc.gov/2021015496

FOR ERIN PALMER

CONTENTS

ACKNOWLEDGMENTS

Part of me knows that I should call this book a "labor of love." This would imply that it was an arduous and painful process that, ultimately, became its own reward. I cannot say that, however, because that would be untrue. Working, thinking, researching, and writing this book has been a truly joyful experience. It has had some low moments, but it has been overwhelmingly thrilling to overcover the life an interpretation can have. Seeing Billy Graham weave into the existing stream of evangelical thought spurred me to see where it went next, and each stone dug out showed ten more stones to uncover. This book is but a snapshot of the life that biblical interpretations can (and do) have. I hope the joy I had in writing it shines through in reading it.

There are so many people to thank, and I am certain I have forgotten someone. Know how grateful I am, even if your name is not here. But the first two people I must thank are Dr. Herbert Marbury and Dr. Annalisa Azzoni of Vanderbilt University. Dr. Azzoni and Dr. Marbury asked me the same question upon leaving my dissertation defense: "What's next?" This book is that "next." I am truly grateful for their wisdom, teaching, and patience. I would also be remiss if I neglected to thank my advisor at Vanderbilt, Dr. C. L. Seow, for sound advice that motivated me to see this project through: "Some scholars read. Other scholars write." Many thanks also to Dr. Fernando Segovia from Vanderbilt, who taught me, when studying how people interpret the Bible, to always ask, "Who, what, why, and for how much?" I am indebted to Dr. Neal Walls from Wake Forest University and Dr. Mark Roncace from Wingate University; you both fanned the flame that led to this moment. Also, a special shout-out to a student from Nebraska Wesleyan University, Alexander Fairchild-Flynn, whose research on Ronald Reagan laid the foundation for chapter 5 in this book.

This book would not be possible without the love of my mom and dad, and my brothers, Thomas and Daniel Redding. You put up with my questions and helped me harness my passions for Christianity, church, and the Bible without letting me forget why I started down this path in the first place. This project also exists due to the wisdom, patience, and needed honesty from Cade Jarrell from Baylor University Press. Cade answered all my emails and helped me shape this wild idea into something that is simultaneously accessible, academically sound, and a wonderful articulation of my ideas. The last acknowledgment goes to my partner and spouse, Erin Palmer. Erin and I met in a graduate religious studies program, and she helped me work through difficult ideas. Quite frankly, she helped make them so much better. This book is what it is because of Erin, and it sits before you today because of so many people that told me to keep working, keep writing, and keep searching.

INTRODUCTION

Blood, Faith, and Country

It's the End of the World as We Know It . . .

In 2019 a billboard advertising a local gun store sparked a national debate. Just outside the rural mountain town of Murphy, North Carolina, a community close to where Billy Graham died, Cherokee Guns advertised its brand alongside pictures of four female Democratic officials. Spread across the advertisement was a message recalling Revelation 6:1-8 and the narrative of the Four Horsemen. It read, "The 4 Horsemen Cometh," but a red line crossed out "Cometh," and "are Idiots" took its place. Responses were, to say the least, politically divisive. When asked about the sign, shop owner Steve "Doc" Wachloz defended his actions: "I'm not inciting any violence or being racist. It's a statement. It's an opinion." He added, "They're socialists, from my point of view. I also feel a couple of them, being Muslim, have ties to actual terrorist groups."[1] The Coalition to Stop Gun Violence responded: "Threats against members of Congress, particularly minority members, are [trending upward] and it is driven by the president's racial rhetoric. This is dangerous!!!"[2]

Both Wachloz and media rhetoric surrounding the billboard noted the ad's interpretation of Revelation, but little did Wachloz and others realize that his reading of Revelation was far from unique, nor was it even truly his own. The Four Horsemen are staples of conspiracy theorists and political enthusiasts alike, with partisan roots dating back to the earliest Christian interpretations of John's Apocalypse. For example, consider the annotations throughout an evangelical mainstay, the Scofield Reference Bible. Published in 1909 and revised in 1917 to wide circulation, the Scofield Bible pushed a "literal but allegorical" reading of Revelation to say that four horses and four riders will not be literal in appearance; rather, their respective essences will manifest in other allegorical but quite marked ways. Even earlier, famed Reformer Martin Luther connected the apocalyptic Four Horsemen with hardline anti-Catholic sentiment and argued that the Four Horsemen represent state persecution through war, bloodshed, scarcity, famine, and pestilence, all of which are brought on by corrupted Catholic leadership. Knowing that Luther interpreted Revelation during the now-seminal falling out between Reformer and Catholic, it becomes clear that Luther's interpretation of the Four Horseman tells us more about Luther's political and religious adversaries than the biblical text itself. Further, though Luther's interpretation appears tamer than the North Carolina sign, the famed Christian Reformer's words are equally political, as he used Revelation in a prideful attempt to mock and deride the Roman Catholic church.

Religious leaders have long tied their use of biblical texts to the political imperatives of their time, meaning that Luther, Scofield, and a gun shop owner in North Carolina are in good company. Christian biblical interpreters, which is to say persons that claim a connection to some branch of the global faith known as Christianity, are notorious for combining specific contexts with how they read the Bible. This combination of texts with contexts becomes more striking when considering how evangelical Christians in the United States of America continue the practice under the guise of objectivity. They frequently claim that their biblical interpretation is *the* one and only reading, while results show quite the opposite, as their respective political, sociocultural, and historical surroundings shape these purported "neutral" interpretations. Evangelicals are far from being alone with this approach to interpretation, as some of the oldest readers across Christian faith spectrums flank their Bibles with their worlds to make one (the Bible) shed light on the other (the world), creating a symbiotic relationship between readers' worlds and their sacred texts. What is noteworthy about the American evangelical execution of this approach is how many readers feign neutrality, as if to say the text itself speaks to them like the conversation between God and Moses in Exodus at the burning bush. Adding to this is the evangelical belief in reading the Bible as holding keys and clues that unlock and understand how world history will unfold. This relationship is highly one sided, as evangelical readers argue that world events do not change their readings—quite the opposite. World events only align with "correct" evangelical readings, as what appears chaotic and beyond recognition becomes clearer and neater when studied alongside evangelical interpretations. In short, for evangelicals, the world changes, but the Bible and its interpretations never waver.

A cursory overview of evangelical preaching and teaching over the last 150 years highlights this phenomenon, as readers change interpretations to fit their historical surroundings. One key voice in the growth and success of American evangelical thinking is that of Billy Graham, an impassioned evangelist who preached all over the globe to convert as many people as he could to his cause. Graham was also an astute and skilled political operative/ player, as his relationship with American presidents was so palpable that he earned monikers like "America's Pastor,"[3] "America's Preacher,"[4] and "Pastor to Presidents."[5] Yet Graham, like so many who preceded him and proceeded from him, held fast to claims of reading the Bible objectively on his way to national and international prominence. Acknowledging the contexts behind and spurring on evangelical biblical interpretation like that of Billy Graham's, showing how American politics can change according to affected interpretations, and tracing how interpretations shape the world at large are why this book exists. Other books follow similar paths, but they often treat political and nationalistic themes in American evangelical interpretations as strange and atypical, when in fact rabid nationalism and undisguised politics popularize these readings and allow them to endure.

Graham's work underlines this political and cultural codependency between nationalism and evangelical interpretation, and his ongoing popularity (even in death) makes his work an ideal case study in tracking how apocalyptic ideas (like those expressed on the North Carolina gun shop's billboard) permeate American culture.

Graham is the definitive example of an American evangelical in word and deed. He changed interpretations and theology according to political and social pressures, as his apocalyptic readings agreed with his evangelical brethren in content. However, Graham's apocalyptic efforts still shape American ideologies, which sets him apart and makes his work compelling. Graham holds considerable historical significance thanks to his ties to politicians, presidents, and other prominent American voices, and this book will show that when an interpretation affects national policy, national policy affects interpretation. This creates self-reinforcing interpretive cycles, as political rhetoric changes to accommodate interpretations while concerned parties change their interpretations to fit political rhetoric.

American nationalism shapes evangelical biblical interpretation: that is the broader issue. Graham's apocalypticism is our entry point. A pressing example of how these two themes are connected is the path that Graham laid out for the phrase "under God" to be legislated into the U.S. Pledge of Allegiance. This book will show how Graham's apocalyptic fervor shaped something that many Americans say daily without any knowledge of where, how, and why it got that way. Through this lens, when someone brings the pledge to a close with "one nation, under God," that person is effectively repeating ideas put there by Graham. The ripple effects of biblical interpretations and the ideas therein will be referred to throughout this book as "receptions," as calling them interpretations is incorrect. Unlike a reception, a biblical interpretation is a much more active and direct interaction between readers, texts, ideas, histories, and contexts, which more forcefully gets carried into interpretive work. A reception analysis like this book's considers the wedding of ideas with texts, as ideas and texts become so intermingled that one cannot see where one ends and the other begins. An example is needed to clarify potential concerns or questions about the nature of "receptions," and one need look no further than the first chapters of the biblical book of Genesis.

What *Is* Reception History?
The Curious Case of Adam, Eve, and Some Fruit

The simplest way to explain biblical reception as presented in this book is to say that biblical interpretations are like duct tape. Engineers design duct tape to be sticky, meaning that it sticks to things and that things stick to it. Drag a piece around a floor or across a room, in the forest, or through a street, and things will inevitably stick. Now imagine taking that single piece of duct tape—with all the fragments, particles, and remnants accrued—and leaving it alone for decades, maybe even centuries. Then picture a stranger finding this duct tape, picking it up, and attempting to figure out what fragments came first, or second, or third. If the stranger knew nothing of its history and origin, the task would be impossible. However, knowing who carried the tape, where that person took it, and why that person was there illuminates what happened to the tape and why. Similarly, readers stick interpretations to texts and reuse them without question, creating a permanent imprint that contemporary readers take for granted as always being there. One such example is the type of fruit Adam and Eve eat in Genesis 3. Hebrew, Greek, and Lain manuscripts of the popular story simply say that the pair eats some "fruit," but the apple has become so synonymous with this story that apples now carry motifs like temptation, lust, and desire. An apple is not inherently a sexual object, nor does Genesis reveal what they bit into; the answers lie beyond both the fruit tree and the document itself, as early Christian interpreters shed light on the apple's possible origins.

Early Christians' readings of Genesis take root through Christian leaders known as the church fathers. These men and their readings shaped contemporary Christianity around the world, for better or worse, and their "fingerprints" cover biblical texts and modern-day interpretations. However, despite considerable spread and continuation of interpretations from the church fathers, the apple is strangely missing. Justin Martyr does not use "apple" to describe the Genesis fruit in his famous *Dialogue with Trypho* (155 CE), nor does Irenaeus of Lyon in his lengthy tome *Against Heresies* (189 CE). Ephrem the Syrian (306–373 CE) wrote concerning many biblical texts and theological issues, including the events in Genesis 1–3, but his work with Genesis refers to the thing that Adam and Eve eat simply as "fruit" and argues that the tree itself attracted Adam and Eve, leading to their downfall and expulsion from Eden.[6]

Like Ephrem, Ambrose of Milan (340–397 CE) weaves his discussion of Adam, Eve, the garden, and the tree into a larger consideration of theological issues and ideas. Ambrose addresses the "fruit of this tree," which is the tree of the knowledge of good and evil, in a writing collection that he calls *Paradise*. The title *Paradise* is a stand-in term for what Ambrose considers humanity's and creation's perfection, and he traces what he perceives as paradise's scriptural branches back to Genesis to understand how and why humanity's choice brought evil into existence.[7] However, the fruit's specifics are inconsequential for Ambrose, as it is merely a vehicle Ambrose uses to explain his understanding of sin.

This metaphorical and allegorical trend begun by Justin Martyr, Irenaeus, and Ambrose continues with John Chrysostom (349–407 CE) and Augustine of Hippo (354–439 CE), as their respective interpretive priorities focus on the relationship between Adam's choice and subsequent fallout from eating the fruit. Chrysostom uses Adam, and not Eve, eating the fruit as a metaphor for his contemporaries and the choices set before them, saying:

> Such is the great evil of failing to stay within the bounds which God fixed for us from the beginning. This is why Adam, in his hope for higher honor, fell from the honor which he had. And the same thing happens in the case of men who have an avaricious love for money. Many of them, many a time, have lost what they had because they wanted more than they had. So also those who think they have the fullness of knowledge here will even lose the partial knowledge proper to this world.[8]

Augustine reads Adam and Eve's choices in the garden as allegory for the Christian church, writing in *City of God*:

> This account can be even better read as an allegory of the Church, prophetical of what was to happen in the future. Thus, the Garden is the Church itself, as we can see from the Canticle of Canticles; the four rivers are the four Gospels; the fruit-bearing trees are the saints, as the fruits are their works; and the tree of life is, of course, the Saint of saints, Christ; and the tree of the knowledge of good and evil is the free choice of our own will.[9]

Early Christian leaders and thinkers read what happens in Genesis 3 with great importance, but each reception's nondescript approach to the fruit shows that specifics bore little or no significance to how and why Christians understood the story.

A consistent thread in these early Christian readings is the overt theologizing each reader puts upon the text. Readings are highly allegorical and insert the events of Genesis into the reader's respective historical context, with each proposing a note of theological significance as they maneuver their contemporary issues into the biblical narrative. Such interpretive moves persist in contemporary twenty-first-century Christian readings, as many

Christian thinkers do not hesitate to read Adam and Eve's simple decision to eat fruit as the bedrock event that sank the world into sin and evil, thus creating a void filled by Jesus of Nazareth.

This reception stream is itself worth many volumes of consideration, but for our purposes, the problem persists: if the "apple" connection did not begin with early Christian interpreters, where did it originate? The answer lies not in the work of Justin Martyr or Ephrem or any other noted Christian thinker; instead, one can simply look to Greek and Roman religious literature. Apples are frequently presented as catalysts for change and the dynamic relationship between the human and divine realms.[10] Thus, at some unknown point, the contexts of first- and second-century Christian interpreters shaped this unknown and unnamed fruit as an apple.

Layout of the Book

A discussion of what the biblical text contains (for example, fruit) compared to what people place upon the text (apple) illuminates that readers have long allowed cultural and social influences to change biblical interpretation. It is very much the norm. Graham, the interpreters that precede him, and those that follow him are not atypical in their approaches to Daniel and Revelation, but what makes Graham unique is that, unlike the apple, one can see the historical connection between American legislation, political use of "under God," and Graham's apocalyptic worldview. Further, one can trace the impact of Graham's apocalyptic rhetoric on President Dwight D. Eisenhower's 1954 legislation (that inserted "under God" into the Pledge of Allegiance) and argue that every time people recite the pledge, they speak Graham's words. This is the task of this book: to trace the journey of Graham's apocalyptic interpretations alongside an analysis of Graham's political power, the trajectory of which still shapes the American political and religious landscape through presidential use of the phrase "one nation, under God."

Chapter 1 starts this journey with an accessible history that examines how Christian interpreters, including Graham, tied nationalism into how they interpret Daniel and Revelation. The chapter's explicit purpose is to show how major Christian interpreters like Justin Martyr, Martin Luther, John Calvin, and many others saw *themselves* as God's chosen people or nation, claimed their enemies were God's enemies, and asserted that Daniel and Revelation offered specific instructions to ensure *their* protection over and against other peoples, nations, and lands. The chapter also illuminates the how and why of the selected Christian apocalyptic interpretations to consider the politics of interpretation and reception that precede American evangelical Christianity.

Chapter 2 shows how Graham's nationalistic flair molded his interpretation of Daniel and Revelation, which in turn made his work a major part of his life and ministry, eventually leading to his greater political and cultural involvement. Post–World War II America was ripe for American evangelical apocalyptic theology and the promises it carried, creating space for Graham to take American Christianity and American politics from interwoven into being inseparable. The chapter consults Graham's own words by analyzing sermons, books, interviews, and other sources for Graham's use and implementation of Daniel and Revelation to reveal the profound significance of apocalyptic thought throughout Graham's work.

Graham's life, work, and subsequent nationalism did not occur in a vacuum. For this reason, chapter 3 dissects the people that influenced Graham's apocalyptic worldview. Graham's nationalistic interpretations built upon earlier Christian thinkers, emphasizing that Graham's content alone does not make his views remarkable. Instead, Graham's presenting of a strong America as good for the world and divine cosmos (alongside strategic political maneuvers) made his brand of apocalyptic nationalism gain traction. Graham's alignments with powerful politicians, paired with America's post–World War II delusion regarding military and nuclear superiority, rocketed him to great fame while also giving him considerable space to preach and teach his views to try to shape America according to his apocalyptic worldview.

Chapter 4 ties everything together and breaks down the political, cultural, and religious moment of President Eisenhower's 1954 legislation of "under God," completing the journey of Graham's interpretation of Daniel and Revelation from pulpit to public. Because of this legislation, "under God" became a vehicle through which Graham pushed a new way of Christian exceptionalism into the national discourse. The chapter details how Graham's continuation of an existing idea, that any nation declaring itself to be "under God" will receive divine blessing and protection, became an unquestioned national ideology recited in schools, homes, sporting events, and other places around the country. It also unpacks how a Scottish Presbyterian minister named George Docherty became infatuated with Graham and the evangelist's idealized America, to show that it was Graham's nationalistic apocalyptic zeal that spurred Docherty to preach a sermon he knew Eisenhower would hear. This very sermon sparked the president to lobby for and ultimately insist upon making "under God" a permanent American adage.

Chapter 5 illuminates where Graham's reception went next, and how it got there through specific political and cultural machinations. This chapter traces the fingerprints and echoes of Graham's work to show how presidents after Eisenhower used "under God" as a political totem or virtue signal to achieve certain political ends and perpetuate their version of an apocalyptic American ideology. The chapter uses presidential administrations as chronological parameters to consider cultural movements and legislation after Graham, showing how the salve Graham saw for the nation and world is now a method of excusing politically contentious decisions.

The conclusion considers possible avenues for further study, as the political moment ushered in by the Trump presidency shows Graham's lasting impact with shocking prejudice. This chapter engages a recent incident of American apocalyptic nationalism and compares the response of Graham's son, Franklin Graham (president/CEO of the Billy Graham Evangelical Association), with the response of another Christian leader to show that political leaders still use Billy Graham's ideas as a bureaucratic tool to control American public opinion. We will consider contemporary receptions of Graham's reception and how they continue the process of reception by further wedding biblical interpretation with political motivation, leading to one conclusion: biblical texts continue to speak only through the wants, needs, and motivations of interpreters.

ONE

ANYTHING BUT EXTRAORDINARY

A Brief History of Apocalyptic Reception

Let the Reader Understand:
The Messages of Daniel and Revelation, Then and Now

One could approach Graham's evangelical nationalism with
scorn, saying that he "destroyed" or "manipulated" the text to
fit his agenda. Yet such an observation would be superficial and,
quite frankly, uninformed. A study of Christians who came before
Graham and other evangelicals shows that readers have long tied
their current political loyalties to biblical texts, with Daniel and
Revelation holding special places in the nationalistic hermeneutical canon. That is the purpose of this chapter: to trace the
thread of interpretative nationalism through the works of Christian writers, including theologians, into the twentieth century. Its
focus is sharp and moves through sources with the singular goal
of showing the palpable thread of personal and communal alle-
giances among early Christians and their interpretations of Daniel and Revelation. These two apocalyptic texts lend themselves to
vastly different interpretive conclusions, as their bizarre imagery
layers violence and political intrigue with divine intervention to

craft narratives that scare away some readers while rolling out a red carpet for others. Political language in Daniel and Revelation creates considerable space for nationalistic flair, into which many Christian readers happily insert themselves and their respective civic circumstances.

Daniel unfolds with striking narrative prose, telling of stubborn Babylonian kings that stumble and flail, barely capable of running their empire. Kings Nebuchadnezzar, Belshazzar, and Darius reign with shocking imprudence, as an Israelite man named Daniel and his three friends consistently undermine government efforts not by force or violence but with faith and dependence on their God. Daniel 1–6 reads like a record on repeat, with each chapter describing a harrowing event or vision that befalls a king and threatens his kingdom, along with a recurring solution that can fix everything and prevent any evil from befalling the leader and his subjects: if the king simply acknowledges Daniel's deity as the one true God, all will be forgiven and prosperity will return to the land. Daniel 7–12 is like a nightmare birthed from the optimism of Daniel 1–6, as Daniel watches the world burn down around him because its people and nations have forgotten their God. Here again, the solution is simple: if the people and their leaders would worship God, the horrors would end and peace would flow across the land.

The New Testament book of Revelation is similar to Daniel 7–12, as a seer witnesses the world being torn to pieces thanks to leaders and nations leading their people astray. Wars rage across the heavens, the world burns, a great satanic beast reigns, and all humanity can do is suffer. And yet, like Daniel, the narrator reminds the reader repeatedly that the cause of such destruction and death is simple: the world, its rulers, and its peoples have rejected their God and therefore suffer the consequences through death and dismay. Revelation ends with a new world, modeled after God's wants and needs, and fashioned around nations and peoples that bow in obedience.

Daniel and Revelation confound and fascinate, prompting readings and receptions that vary from subdued and subversive to outlandish and hysterical. Yet historical Christian readings of Daniel and Revelation unwittingly reveal something quite striking: that the tying of the reader's concurrent social, political, and cultural contexts to the fulfillment of both Daniel and Revelation goes inevitably unquestioned. Christians claim to read "neutrally" but are heavily (and quite consistently) influenced by their social and political contexts. Readers inserting themselves into the text and its subsequent interpretation is nothing new, nor is it inherently off-base; what makes it unique for our study is how quickly and consistently exegetical paths lead to unapologetic nationalism.

Early Christianity through Late Antiquity

Justin Martyr (100–165) lived and worked in the Roman Empire, and his *Dialogue with Trypho* is one of the earliest Christian interactions with Daniel and Revelation that reads the two books together as if they were telling one story. Martyr believes that a reader needs Revelation to interpret Daniel, and though Martyr does not explicitly say that the fourth beast and the antichrist are one and the same, he uses Daniel 7 to understand the second beast of Revelation 13 as an antimessianic figure.[1] Martyr jumps from the text to his world to make his antichrist a political threat that will speak blasphemous words and mislead people from God, and ultimately put the human world at risk. Such a reading lays the foundation upon which other Christians work as they rebuild and re-create biblical enemies as their foes while painting themselves as salvific. According to Martyr, he and others like him are the people that God needs to defeat these foretold enemies. It remains up to them what side they will choose.

Priest Irenaeus of Lyon (130–202) continued Martyr's tactic and read Daniel through Revelation, going so far as to quote Martyr in *Against Heresies* while arguing that God maintains total control over human governments: "Earthly rule, therefore, has been appointed by God for the benefit of nations and not by the Devil."[2] This position warrants considerable discussion and thought. One could argue that Irenaeus wants to provide meaning and purpose to his audience as they consider the place of government within the fledgling Christian faith. Conversely, one could just as easily argue that Irenaeus' stance merely justifies decisions made by persons in power. But what matters here is that Irenaeus takes what he reads from Daniel and Revelation and applies it to his world and his government, saying that the books speak directly to his current situation. It is also noteworthy how readily Irenaeus uses two apocalyptic books that speak at length about God striking down then replacing corrupted governments to advocate for supporting the current governing system. Like Martyr, Irenaeus does not see himself (or others like him) as the "bad guy" while situating himself in a position of moral and political superiority. He is, for all intents and purposes, the one meant to call out improper behavior in others and not within himself.

Irenaeus' apparent nationalistic complacency contrasts with Hippolytus of Rome (170–235) and his staunchly anti-Roman stance. Like Martyr and Irenaeus, Hippolytus read Daniel and Revelation as one narrative to find hope amid persecution and suffering inflicted by the Roman government. Unlike Irenaeus, Hippolytus railed against what he considered to be church hypocrisy following the increase and spread of Christianity during the late second and early third centuries. Daniel's enemies become metaphorical representations of the Roman Empire, leaving space for Hippolytus to argue that secular government influence contaminates faith.[3] Hippolytus believes that human choices influence divine and human realms because, according to his interpretation, as humans conquer and rule, the world turns closer to what Daniel and Revelation foretell.

Hippolytus' solution is increased Christian martyrdom, which creates an ideology of apocalyptic political sacrifice.[4] It becomes Christians' duty to sacrifice themselves against corrupted governments, making it better to die a martyr than live in corrupt subservience. His clear displeasure with the Church and its allegiance with Rome uncovers a nationalistic tension lurking beneath the surface: Hippolytus only opposes Rome's influence on the church because he believes that Rome has lost its way. Unlike Irenaeus, who presents all governments as ordained by God, Hippolytus sees the Roman Empire as a fallen kingdom, the likes of which God reduces to ashes in Daniel and Revelation. Should Rome, or any nation for that matter, correct its course and welcome Christians with open arms, then Hippolytus would sing a different tune, as any government's treatment of Christianity is paramount to determining its health, vitality, and prosperity.

Hippolytus-inspired government opposition held sway into the fourth century. Ephrem the Syrian (306–373) crafted a direct and political polemic with his apocalyptic interpretation, arguing that the fourth beast in Daniel 7 is "Alexander, king of the Greeks," and that the beast's iron teeth are "Alexander's powerful armies, which nearly subdued all kings."[5] Eusebius Hieronymus, more popularly known as Jerome (347–420), also tied Daniel and Revelation to the Roman Empire and claimed their dominion will soon end.[6] Jerome then offered his interpretation of the military history leading to Alexander's rise to power, saying that the leopard's four wings in Daniel 7 emphasize the conqueror's quick and efficient victories, as he was "not simply fighting battles but winning decisive victories."[7] Both Ephrem and Jerome read the apocalyptic books as a roadmap to understanding their respective national and political situations, with the thread of "context shaping content" running strong and unquestioned. This approach has long been so ingrained that one cannot find where the narratives of Daniel and Revelation end and the worlds of the interpreters begin; a self-reinforcing interpretive circle begun by Justin Martyr rolled on into Augustine of Hippo (354–430) and Theodoret of Cyrus (393–458).

The Germanic Visigoths laid siege to Rome in 410 and sent shockwaves throughout the Roman Empire, as its peoples had felt invulnerable to such attacks. Many factors led to the successful sacking of Rome, including, according to interpretation, long-term fallout from dividing the empire after Alexander the Great's death in 323 BC and further division that came following the death of Theodosius I in 395 CE. However, some Roman citizens sought a more immediate scapegoat and lashed out against the empire's newfound infatuation with Christianity, claiming that abandoning their allegiance to Roman gods brought divine wrath upon the city. Such backlash prompted Augustine to pen his seminal *City of God*, in which he argued that all human history is an ongoing war between God and the devil. Central to Augustine's thesis is the highly nationalistic idea of God using governments and the Catholic Church to take down governments and military forces siding with the devil.

Augustine justifies the damage brought upon Rome by reading Daniel and Revelation with an overt Christian nationalism, claiming that the Visigoth attack on Rome is a good thing, a sign of the Roman Empire's piety: "Be he who reads [Daniel], even half asleep, cannot fail to see that the kingdom of the Antichrist shall fiercely, though for a short time, assail the Church before the last judgment of God shall introduce the eternal reign of the saints."[8] Augustine straddles a fine line in *City of God* between imperial complacency and criticism of government by crafting an extended discussion about how the ideal government must mold itself according to God's will and standards. Doing so, he argues, will yield divine prosperity upon the nation and its people, while rejecting God and siding with the demonically corrupted "World" can bring only certain doom. In short, Augustine's lengthy tome presents a familiar argument that is far from unique: the government that sides with God may experience earthly turmoil, but the long-term goals make that worthwhile. Thus, instead of returning to the Roman deities of the pre-Christian era, Augustine lobbies for making the empire *more* Christian to ensure divine protection, based in part on his interpretation of Daniel and Revelation.

Theodoret of Cyrus (393–457) wrote against the background of internal church squabbles in the Eastern Roman Empire that arose from the very same ongoing government upheaval that influenced Augustine's *City of God*. Theodoret, in a book-length dissection of Daniel, ties the four-way division of Alexander the Great's empire to the four beasts in Daniel 7. He also continues the thread of reading Revelation into Daniel, arguing that the final horn upon the fourth beast in Daniel 7 is the antichrist and that the historical trajectory begun in Daniel will culminate in real time according to the events of Revelation. Rome remains the interpretive focus for Theodoret, meaning that Rome's successes and failures determined the fate of both the world and cosmos. According to this thread, God makes the cosmos rise and fall according to Rome's choices. What is remarkable here is that as early as the fourth and fifth centuries, the unquestioned assumption among Roman Christian interpreters aligns with Theodoret's reception of Rome as the center of the biblical world, the human sphere, and the divine realm.

Roman instability in the fourth and fifth centuries was a mere harbinger of what was to come with the rise of Islam in the seventh and eighth centuries. The Muslim world produced a formidable adversary for once-unquestioned Roman political and religious dominance, but most important for tracing the thread of Christian nationalism in apocalyptic literature is the profound effect this global shift had on interpretations. Islamic military and political success shows that as dominant political powers shift, so too do interpretations. Spanish monk and theologian Beatus of Liébana (730–800) incorporated Daniel to explain Revelation, as his interpretation reflected the era's apocalyptic anxieties over Islam to create an elaborate eschatological chronology that stretches throughout the Bible.

Beatus wrote amid the fallout of the Muslim conquest of the Iberian Peninsula that began in 711 before Beatus was even born. According to Beatus, the beasts of Daniel and Revelation represent the Muslim caliphate, and Babylon the Great is now the

Muslim stronghold in Cordova. He interweaves anti-Muslim sentiment to establish the earthly origins of these biblical metaphors and emphasize the all-encompassing reach of destructive world powers, which, if left unchecked, can threaten all of existence. Beatus' interpretation changes the game, as he says that earthly evil can and does threaten the divine realm to create a reciprocal relationship between humans and God. Now God's very reign is at stake, and if Roman Christians do not rise to stop the Muslim threat, Beatus believes that all of creation could fall.

From the Crusades to the Doorstep of the Reformation

Pope Urban II's 1095 call to attack Muslim-occupied Jerusalem (all while his safety in Rome was guaranteed) sent shockwaves throughout the Jewish, Christian, and Muslim worlds as it launched Urban II from prominent religious figure to global political juggernaut.[9] This period also marked a shift in the relationship between Christian and Jew, as each created separate but still highly nationalistic narratives and hermeneutical models to explain the violence and death that tore the region, its people, and their faith traditions apart.[10]

Christian theologian Andrew of St. Victor (1110–1175) rejected any semblance of neutrality as he consulted Jewish interpreters to manipulate their work and openly relate Daniel and Revelation to his own time. He reads the apocalyptic beasts as imperial Rome but argues that Daniel and Revelation are not magical talismans that people can use to understand hidden knowledge about the future. Instead, they merely illustrate how history will unfold: God enters history to thwart apocalyptic evil while establishing an earthly kingdom through earthly means for people that God will deem holy.[11] Andrew's religious and historical contexts underline his interpretive motivations as he borrows heavily from Jewish readers and Jerome, creating an interpretation so bound by preceding interpretations that Andrew, in thinking he reads the text literally, repackages earlier work and continues the Christian trends of reading Daniel's apocalyptic visions as a lens for Christ's return in the book of Revelation. Previous interpretations are so ingrained that Andrew, a highly skilled Hebraist and theologian, cannot see the proverbial hermeneutical forest for the trees.

Catholic Saint Hildegard of Bingen (1098–1179) provides an interesting case study in nationalistic interpretation, as her book *Scivias* described her personal visions of the apocalypse instead of a standard biblical commentary or interpretation. Hildegard claimed to witness a vision accompanied by a disembodied voice from heaven offering an explanation in which she sees five differently colored beasts—a fiery dog, a yellow lion, a pale horse, a black pig, and a gray wolf—bringing terror upon the earth.[12] The vision includes a multicolored man that resembles the statue from Daniel 2, the body of which represents the church, thereby making the Catholic Church itself an agent of evil and corruption. Hildegard's vision reworks biblical apocalypses and uses elements from both Daniel and Revelation to show that she does not simply interpret a text; rather, in her illustration, the ideas take on a life of their own. Hildegard claims no scriptural dependence, despite pervasive echoes of Daniel and Revelation throughout her work and argues that the church itself carries great internal evil. Thus, nations and their leaders lose their way and suffer God's wrath because the church itself decays from corruption. Hildegard wrote in the twelfth century, a period marked by the Second Crusade (1147–1150) and the church's anti-heretical stance that eventually gave way to systemic medieval inquisitions.[13] Further, Hildegard saw the church as caught in a spiral of dramatic decline and blamed clergy as both negligent and lazy.[14] Here the church's primary apocalyptic enemy is the church itself, losing its way and leading followers and, in turn, government systems toward utter destruction.

Unlike Hildegard, Joachim of Fiore (1135–1202) returned this interpretive thread to the biblical text and read the fourth beast in Daniel 7 as the Babylonian Empire and the final horn as the antichrist from Revelation. He withheld specific historical labels for the antichrist but does say that it worked in Rome during his lifetime.[15] Christ's imminent return, preceded by an antichrist that lives in Joachim's temporal and civil contexts, continues the nationalistic tenet of this thread. Just as Joachim believes reading Daniel without Revelation is very wrong, so too is considering that the antichrist and other apocalyptic harbingers would manifest anywhere other than the interpreter's immediate purview.[16]

Nicholas of Lyra (1270–1349) engaged Jewish exegesis from ancient rabbis through his Christian contemporaries, including the great Jewish exegete Rashi.[17] Like Rashi, Nicholas sought plain or literal meanings, but Nicholas also followed the work and method of St. Thomas Aquinas in using metaphors to explain his readings.[18] Nicholas' reading of Daniel and Revelation's apocalyptic beast's is swift and direct: "Bestia qaurta. Romanu Imperium," meaning "The Fourth Beast. The Roman Empire."[19] Nicholas' blunt approach stems from his traumatic time as a Franciscan monk, in which Catholic leadership felt threatened by the order's autonomy and responded with more forceful papal oversight.[20] Nicholas' writings bear tensions of both the Roman Catholic Church and the Roman Empire (during the thirteenth and fourteenth centuries) as each scrambled to recover lost glory while suffering the mistakes of previous leaders. His interpretations reflect this political instability as he focuses on Alexander's divided empire and assigns a kingdom to each beast in Daniel 7: Egypt first, then Syria, followed by Asia, and finally Greece.[21] As the work continues, Nicholas cites Daniel's language of "most terrible" and "more terrifying," which he connects to Revelation, the antichrist, and the church itself, all the while blending religiosity with nationalism. Since, from Nicholas' perspective, both the church and the empire were failing, the cosmic end times had finally arrived. Tying the Roman Empire and Roman Catholic Church together as one adversarial force is unique as it creates an apocalyptic relationship in which the sufferings and faults of one affect the other.[22] Previous iterations of apocalyptic Christian nationalism paint the church as an unwavering moral beacon that a crumbling nation could use to rebuild itself. Now the rot of evil and corruption infect the entire human realm, leaving no other option than to prepare for Jesus' return.

Friar St. Vincent Ferrer (1350–1419) wrote against the backdrop of the fourteenth-century Catholic Western Schism when the Roman Church split into three pieces and each faction claimd the one true pope.[23] War and violence escalated as the divisions vied for control, leaving Christian leaders and laypersons confused and listless. Thus, it was reasonable for someone like devoted friar Vincent to revisit biblical texts that foretell a destructive figure that would build a new order upon the ashes of the old. Seeing the fallen Roman Empire alongside the splintered church, Vincent interweaves Daniel, Revelation, the antichrist, and the Catholic Western Schism into one unified apocalyptic omen.[24] Daniel's four beasts become four papal schisms, with the fourth beast being the fourteenth-century schism, meaning that the current church calamities are the final movement that will usher in the antichrist. Vincent believes national corruption is unchecked and bleeds into the church, creating a theological vacuum in which God has to step to prevent further damage.

Yet in 1412 Vincent changed his reading after making "The Report on the Antichrist" for Pope Benedict XIII.[25] Vincent identifies the fourth beast as the Roman Empire, casts the ten horns as extensions of that empire, then assigns each horn with one of ten schisms to predict the imminent coming of the antichrist. Most important is that Vincent writes this report according to Benedict's blessing, which explains why Vincent makes the work of Benedict the tenth schism but does not blame the papal figure.[26] He blatantly changes his interpretation to appease someone in power, a move that other Christians would replicate and perfect. Vincent sees the situation as an opportunity to increase his political capital and, in so doing, makes the text fit his priorities. The nation now carries blame for looming destruction, as Vincent elevates the church back to its unquestioned position of power.

Christian Receptions from the Reformation

The Protestant Reformation rocketed apocalyptic interpretation beyond Catholic purviews into broader public domains through pastors, deacons, and laypersons offering their readings alongside scholars, including linguists. Apocalyptic nationalism became a benchmark of Protestant thought as leaders like Martin Luther and John Calvin tied Revelation and Daniel to their political and religious contexts. But what they wrote remains far from unique as they built upon, sometimes openly, previous Christian receptions. Luther initially opposed historically focused readings of Daniel and Revelation, but surrounding historical events made him reconsider.[27] The Ottoman Turks' siege of Vienna in 1529 under Suleiman the Magnificent prompted Luther to translate Daniel for insight regarding the political upheaval, which led him to believe that the toes of the statue in Daniel 2 represented his generation.[28] Luther's interpretations carve a unique path, one that will eventually fall under the label of Evangelical Christianity, as his reading is profoundly Christian, highly nationalistic, and built upon a staunchly anti-papal orientation.[29] Luther believes prophetic fulfillments occur readily, and he builds upon Jerome by relating the advancing Ottoman armies and God's final earthly salvation via metaphorical correspondences between each animal in Daniel 7 and the historical kingdoms of Babylon, Medo-Persia, Greece, and Rome.[30] He adds interpretative nuance by reading Daniel's fourth beast and Revelation's antichrist as symbolizing the same thing: the destructive power wielded by the Turkish Empire and the pope.[31] Luther combines Daniel and Revelation to cast the pope, menacing Turkish forces, and the antichrist as justifying personal grievances and to relate them to primordial chaotic evil.[32] Given Luther's position as Protestant Reformer, it makes sense for him to claim that the pope is the antichrist because, according to Luther, the Catholic leader changes laws that Jesus himself established. His interpretation gets very specific, arguing that the pope is the ruler from Daniel 11:36-37 that will "exalt himself and magnify himself above every god."[33] These unambiguous motives become clearer when read alongside Luther's biases or views of German superiority that saturate his receptions. He recreates the Bible's apocalyptic timeline to revolve around German superiority and argues that devout Germans are the saints that the fourth beast and the antichrist fail to deceive.[34] Luther also reads Daniel's imperial succession as predicting that Germany will survive and replace the Jewish people to become God's protected and chosen society. The Reformer lays his staunch anti-Semitism bare as now the apocalyptic books exist to soothe and inspire Christians in times of turmoil with no positive Jewish or Catholic connections.[35] To Luther, Daniel (and the entire Hebrew Bible) exists only to clarify the book of Revelation and herald Christ's return. He goes to great lengths to make Daniel a Christian book, and he traces it through additional New Testament writings, including the Gospel of Matthew, specifically Matthew 24:15, saying the pope is the "abomination of desolation" that Daniel describes in Daniel 9:27 and 12:11.[36] He continues:

> The pope is a god on earth over everything heavenly, earthly, spiritual, and secular and all on his own. No one is permitted to say to him: "What are you doing?" This is the abomination and stench of which Christ speaks in Matthew 24.[37]

Daniel becomes Luther's highest and best prophet because "his work was not only to prophesy of Christ, like the others, but also to count the times and years, determine them, and fix them with certainty."[38]

Luther's anti-Semitic nationalistic tilt is profoundly troubling, as he sees papal corruption spurred by Jewish influence giving way to a period of divinely ordained global German rule.[39] Luther's focus on Germany creates a narrow and highly jingoist apocalyptic perspective, as German supremacy becomes the unavoidable culmination of history. All kingdoms rise and fall to make way for German prosperity. Luther defines his interpretations according to his time and place, and his German-centric agenda taints his work. However, by identifying the adversarial figures of Daniel and Revelation as his enemies, Luther continues the historical and literary trend of Christian nationalism and self-advancement by painting himself and fellow Germans as God's eventual victors.

Responses to Luther and his work were predictably polarizing: labeling the pope, an individual that many considered to be humanity's best connection to God, as the antichrist warranted blowback. For example, twelve years after Luther published his "95 Theses," German humanist Johannes Cochlaeus called Luther the antichrist in the pamphlet "Seven Heads of Luther, Eight High Things of the Christian Faith." Hans Brosamer worked with Cochlaeus on this project and made a woodcut image depicting Luther as the seven-headed beast of Revelation 12–13 (fig.1).[40] Each head bears a different label—Doctor, Martinus, Luther, Clergyman, Enthusiast, Visitor, and Barabbas—making Luther a hydra-headed adversary bearing the trappings of a trusted leader destined to destroy the Christian church. Someone on Luther's side did not take kindly to Brosamer's woodcut and responded anonymously with "The Seven-Headed Papal Beast" (fig. 2).[41] This piece features the cross overladen with a sign that reads, "A sack full of Indulgences for cash," a direct jab at the church's indulgences practice. The response and Brosamer's woodcut both parody the popular image of the Mass of St. Gregory published in 1476, with the Protestant response mirroring the piece so well that a casual viewer may confuse the satirical take for the 1476 original.[42] The ping-ponging back and forth between Luther, his supporters, and his critics shows how openly Christians moved themselves and their enemies in and out of the biblical texts and its interpretations, prompting one to wonder why any author bothered to attempt neutrality or objectivity with their work.[43] This sequence of events unleashed a cascade of Christian

FIG. 1 "MARTINUS LUTHER SIEBENKOPFF"
Woodcut from *Septiceps Lutherus: ubiq[ue] sibi, suis scriptis, co[n]trari[us], invisitatione[m] Saxonica[m]* (1529), https://commons.wikimedia.org/wiki/File:Martinus_Luther_Siebenkopff.jpg

FIG. 2 "THE SEVEN-HEADED PAPAL BEAST"

Anonymous woodcut, sixteenth century, https://commons.wikimedia
.org/wiki/File:The_seven_headed_pope_beast.jpg

nationalism that now pitted Protestants against Catholics, paving the way for further division within the Protestant movement and its apocalyptic foundations.

John Calvin (1509–1564) did not write full commentaries on Revelation or Daniel. He did, however, give a series of lectures in 1561 that focus on Daniel as "both an exemplary man of faith and prophet revealing God's word and plan for the future."[44] He receives the trend of reading Daniel's four beasts as four empires and engages Daniel 7 with confidence until he reaches the fourth beast, claiming, "This Fourth Monarchy is more difficult" compared to the preceding three.[45] He addresses this difficulty and discusses possible explanations, including reading the fourth beast as Rome, the pope, and what he calls "the Turkish kingdom."[46] Unlike Luther and preceding interpretations, Calvin reads Daniel as *ex eventu prophecy* and argues that Daniel 2 and 7 "represent kingdoms and situations that are long past."[47] Calvin also argues that Scripture is intentionally allegorical so that God could create "a kind of living image" that can change according to reader, time, and place.[48] Such an acknowledgment shows Calvin's awareness of readers changing their interpretation to fit their situation, a bold move that he couches with a concession of his own: "I do not doubt that [Daniel] is shown the figure of the Roman Empire," and "I do not doubt that the little horn can be understood as Julius Caesar and the others after him, namely, Augustus, Tiberius, Caligula, Claudius, Nero, and others."[49] His approach is a "both-and" of sorts, as it allows Daniel and Revelation to speak to their respective eras *and* connect to a given reader's social and political backdrop. He makes it *his* while also showing that many others have done the same.

Calvin's accompanying theological analysis pairs this flexible certainty with a dissenting perspective on the coming apocalypse: its advent is soon, but it will not occur in his lifetime.[50] He reads the Roman Empire as cruel and self-destructive, as symbolized by the statue in Daniel 2. However, Calvin interprets Rome's decline as an appropriate conclusion to its misguided political machinations and not due to divine intervention. Rome does not fall because of divine punishment; rather, it falls because of internal corruption, which the divine punishment in Daniel and Revelation represents.[51] This generalized approach is wrapped in nationalistic political motives while also reflecting the separation between Protestant Christianity and the Roman Catholic Church. Protestant leaders like Luther and Calvin had the opportunity to unshackle Christianity from any national or governmental affiliation, as the relationship between the Roman government and the Catholic Church created a symbiotic relationship that enabled the faith to flourish while also entrapping the church in Roman political intrigue. However, in aligning apocalyptic imagery with Rome, Calvin and Luther fell into this much-maligned political intrigue as their disdain toward the church reflects their displeasure with countries and governments beyond their own. Luther championed German superiority to a fault, and Calvin spoke out against perceived "unholy" government forces after he fled his native France for his adopted home of Switzerland. In short, every government that opposed Protestantism at its advent was considered corrupt and evil, while those that supported the movement became beacons of cosmological civil stability.

Like Protestant Reformers and select Catholic readers before him, Swiss Reformer Heinrich Bullinger (1504–1575) reads the fourth beast as the Roman Empire because the beast and Rome are "terrible and horrible."[52] He argues the empire's reach is almost inescapable, as nations that never physically see Rome nonetheless suffer from its cruelty, greed, and subsequent dissolution. Unlike Christian readings that flatter by finding redeeming qualities in the empire, Bullinger sees Rome as thoroughly terrible.[53] His insistence on the fourth beast as Rome, despite the changing tides of history, creates a hermeneutical bridge between the empire of Alexander the Great, Alexander's predecessors, and the rise of the papal Roman Empire. The constant reality of Rome's power allows for historical flexibility between Daniel and Revelation, binding the two together in an interpretive circle. He acknowledges previous Christian readings that interpret the fourth beast as Islamic adversaries but points to Rome as an ongoing celestial evil. This is remarkable because of Bullinger's choice to acknowledge, then reject, anti-Islamic readings, thereby stressing a broader chronological worldview that focuses on God's long-term work across history.

German theologian and musician Nikolaus Selnecker (1530–1592) wrote *Der Prophet Daniel, und die Offenbarung Johannis* to discuss Daniel, Revelation, and each book's relationship to the other and to label both Islam and the Catholic Church as the collective enemy of Christianity and Germany. Previous interpreters have a considerable impact on Selnecker's reading: Daniel's vision of the four beasts in Daniel 7 is a prophecy focusing on the kingdom of Christ, each creature representing one of the monarchies presented in Daniel 2, and the fourth beast is the Roman Empire with the horns representing kingdoms that split from larger imperial entities.[54] Selnecker then unites anti-Islamic and anti-Catholic interpretations by arguing that Revelation is a revision of Daniel and claiming that Daniel foretells the rise of Islam while Revelation describes the corrupted church.[55] He becomes even more political when he claims that the pope is as dangerous to Christianity as the prophet Muhammad, and that history will continue repeating itself unless "true" Christians (that is, those cut from Selnecker's German cloth) intervene. Selnecker's composite figure of Islam and the pope lacks biblical evidence, but despite this he persists and shapes his interpretation according to his German Protestant worldview with little regard for the text.

Like Selnecker, Johannes Oecolampadius (1482–1531) received considerable scrutiny from his peers and others who accepted the work of Luther, Calvin, and Philip Melanchthon as the definitive readings of Daniel and Revelation. Calvin openly criticized Oecolampadius by making disparaging remarks about Oecolampadius' apocalyptic chronology, calling it "loose and inaccurate."[56] Despite criticisms, Oecolampadius did what his peers did in reading Daniel and Revelation as divine codebreakers for contemporary social and political realities.[57] As with Luther, Oecolampadius' work contains overt anti-Jewish sentiment that manifests in reading both Testaments as intended for Christian audiences, which carries particular irony as his exegetical approach relies on his dedication as a Hebrew student.[58] He reads Daniel as a prophetic figure, and his Revelation interpretation aligns with other Christian interpreters. Daniel 7's little horn is the antichrist and the horn's "blasphemous words" at Daniel 7:11 connect to Revelation, the dragon, and "the devil himself." Further, Oecolampadius reads the fourth beast as Muhammad and its ten horns as Muslim military leaders.[59] Oecolampadius is steadfast in his approach and argues his reading is literal and his work objective when he places anti-Islamic and anti-Jewish perspectives in Daniel and creates a direct lineage from Daniel's visions through Revelation.

Summation

This overview shows how Christian interpreters made Daniel and Revelation fit their geographical, religious, and social milieus despite no direct textual evidence to support these claims. Anytime anyone cited a text, it was only to support their interpretive agenda, creating a self-reinforcing loop of skewed interpretation. The growth of Christianity, the persistence of Judaism, and the rise of Islam forced Christians to resolve the place of Hebrew Scriptures alongside the New Testament. Similarly, Christian authors adjusted the identity of Daniel 7's fourth beast and Revelation's antichrist according to their own respective primary adversaries, ranging from Muslims and Jews to the pope and Protestant Reformers. These Christians made Daniel and Revelation companion pieces, and in so doing constructed a supersessionist apocalyptic worldview that replaced Israelite history with self-fulfilling Christian prophecies of redemption.

The chapter began with Justin Martyr and his *Dialogue*, a work that set the standard for succeeding apocalyptic interpreters, whereby a final cataclysmic figure was given a messianic mantle and the foundation was laid for connecting Daniel's Son of Man with Revelation's Jesus. Irenaeus' reading was much like

Martyr's in content and intent, especially as Irenaeus read Daniel 7 and Revelation as one prophetic narrative. Hippolytus continued the tradition of reading Daniel and Revelation together and cited the direct influence of Irenaeus, which, in turn, highlighted the influence of Justin Martyr.[60] What is most important for us is that Hippolytus, Irenaeus, and Justin Martyr each believed their reading was true, literal, and grounded solely on the biblical texts. Further, none dared to critique Scripture; they were just as quick to defend biblical historical integrity as they were to change their readings according to personal whims. Thus, reading Daniel and Revelation became an act of juggling history, method, and historical trajectory that loaded the text itself down with inseparable interpretive baggage. On the one hand, Daniel and Revelation were still read as offering insight into the divine's role in human history, a constant upon which Christians readers found hermeneutical rest. Conversely, when history failed to reflect what Daniel and Revelation "said," interpreters reinterpreted as necessary to fit the political and social moment.

Fallout from the Protestant Reformation radically changed the spread of different and unique readings of Daniel, Revelation, and their apocalyptic content. Theories of divine kingship and religious revolution resonated with early Protestant theologians, causing interpretive trends to continue into Renaissance literature and Enlightenment philosophies. As the Catholic Church and Protestant Reformers accepted one another's permanence, a new enemy in Enlightenment rationalism emerged. This changed biblical criticism forever as reason and logic, rather than the church or human empires, would become the adversarial figure against which church leaders fought for power. These changing historical tides and their visible impact on interpretation uncovered a pattern that continued through Billy Graham's reading of Daniel and Revelation: Christian readers made the Bible fit their era with little thought for the fact that other Christians did just that all while history rolled on and none of their apocalyptic interpretations came true.

TWO

THE ROOTS OF GRAHAM'S APOCALYPTIC NATIONALISM

Where to Begin?

Finding where and how an idea started is difficult, if not impossible. History has "eureka!" moments that people point to as "when it all began," but for every moment of clarity that sparks innovation, or each time someone puts pen-to-paper for the next earth-shattering concept, there are countless hours and numerous others that led to it. For example, scholars spend lifetimes studying the global evolution of languages and seek the first iteration of a word or letter. The reality of such work is bittersweet, as the more one pursues such work, the more one sees its evasiveness. No matter how old they are, written ideas, words, and letters simply demonstrate when someone decides or merely has the capacity to write something down or pass it along; it does not mean it is the first or original.

With that in mind, an exact and comprehensive discussion of apocalyptic ideas that crosses each "t" and dots every "i" is nearly impossible. One can, however, trace historical streams and uncover when an idea becomes popular, or at the very least discern where that idea and a person intersect. This is the case with Billy Graham and his American-centric apocalyptic theology. He did not invent American exceptionalist ideas, but he did perfect and spread their influence into the nation's highest rungs of power to cement the idea of "America as a Christian nation" among evangelical voters. Therefore, considering the people that influenced Graham and examining their work with Daniel and Revelation illuminates where Graham got the ideas necessary to craft his version of America's apocalyptic trajectory.

The Roots: Dispensationalism

Graham and the modern evangelical movement have many roots, but John Nelson Darby (1800–1882) and Cyrus Ingerson Scofield (1843–1931) are noteworthy titans of American apocalyptic Christianity in the nineteenth and early twentieth centuries, and their fingerprints cover Graham's apocalyptic worldview. Their similar approaches to biblical scholarship helped define Christian biblical interpretation of their era. Their work also shaped Graham in considerable and profound ways. Darby bears the standard for Christian movements known as dispensationalism and futurism, which gained considerable traction in the United States following the 1909 publication of Scofield's widely known and highly profitable *Scofield Reference Bible*. True to the form of this book, Scofield took Darby's ideas and developed them, building so much upon Darby that it is difficult to tell where Darby's work ends and Scofield's begins. And yet, despite their prominent place in American apocalyptic Christianity, neither Darby nor Scofield's ideas are fully their own. Both build upon ideas from and sermons by an English Calvinist named John Edwards.

Edwards, not to be confused with the North American revivalist Jonathan Edwards, was born in Hertford, England, in 1637 and died in 1716. He preached many sermons and taught lessons on Christian topics that included theology, ecclesiology, and biblical studies. In 1699, Edwards published *A Compleat History or Survey of All the Dispensations*, a massive tome in which he dissects human history and divides it into different segments called "dispensations." This type of theological perspective, called "dispensationalism," reads Daniel and Revelation as biblical keystones that show God's plan for history according to segments of time set aside for certain purposes. Edwards uses dispensationalism to create an apocalyptic biblical timeline that relies heavily on interpreting all Christian and Hebrew Scriptures through Daniel and Revelation. He claims that his interpretive approach is literal, arguing that Jesus will reign from heaven after a physical, bodily return as foretold in Daniel 7:14. Edwards dives deeper into Daniel and writes that he has "undertaken a Great Work, to display all the Transactions of Divine Providence relating to the Methods of Religion, from the Creation of Genesis to the end of the World, from the first chapter of Genesis to the last of the Revelation."[1] In short, Edwards sees himself as burdened with a mighty and wonderous task as he works to understand how these ancient books can shed light on global affairs.

Edwards crafts a historical timeline based on his biblical interpretation to situate his time and place near its end:

I. Innocence and Felicity, or Adam created upright
II. Sin and Misery, Adam fallen
III. Reconciliation, or Adam recovered, from
    Adam's redemption to the end of the world
    A. Patriarchal economy
        1. Adamical, antediluvian (pre-flood)
        2. Noahical post-flood
        3. Abrahamick
    B. Mosaical economy
    C. Gentile (concurrent with A and B)
    D. Christian or Evangelical
        1. Infancy, primitive period, past
        2. Childhood, present period
        3. Manhood, future (millennium)
        4. Old age, from the loosing of
           Satan to the conflagration[2]

This layout conveniently weaves Edwards' lifetime alongside major biblical events like the flood, the exodus, and the birth of Christ. Like those who come before and so many who will come after, Edwards reshapes history to fit his narrative interpretation and plants himself and his generation firmly on the cusp of Jesus' return. The interpretive logic here is simple: how *he* reads Scripture shows *him* the truth, as Edwards builds upon an unapologetic self-reinforcing interpretive circle. Every book in the Bible exists to help Edwards understand his place in history, with Daniel and Revelation being distinct maps to the how and when of Jesus' return. This sets the standard for future dispensationalists, including Darby and Scofield, as Edwards repeats and cites Scripture to support his claims without offering evidence beyond arguing that his interpretation is operative. This is how *he* reads Scripture, which suffices for him and boldly represents Protestant individualism: what matters most in biblical interpretation is the relationship between the reader, the text, and God.

Hymn writer Isaac Watts (1674–1748) picked up where Edwards left off, as his work connects Edwards to Darby through an outline of history that will become a dispensational paradigm. Compared to that of Edwards, Watts' dispensational history is much simpler and more direct:

I. The Dispensation of Innocence, or the Religion of Adam at first

II. The Adamical Dispensation of the Covenant of Grace, or the Religion of Adam after his Fall

III. The Noah Dispensation, or the Religion of Noah

IV. The Abraham Dispensation, or the Religion of Abraham

V. The Moses Dispensation, or the Jewish Religion

VI. The Christian Dispensation[3]

Watts speaks about the millennium era following his sixth dispensation, but he does not consider it to be another dispensation; for him, it is simply history's culmination. Thus, Watts limits himself to six dispensations. Darby follows Watts' simpler lead with his own dispensational timeline but chooses to include the millennium as a seventh tier:

I. Paradisaical state to the Flood
II. Noah
III. Abraham
IV. Israel
    A. Under the law
    B. Under the priesthood
    C. Under the kings
V. Gentiles
VI. The Spirit
VII. The Millennium[4]

Educated at Trinity College, Dublin, Darby took his Edwards- and Watts-inspired dispensations across the United States and Canada in the early nineteenth century. Darby's missionary travels sparked general interest in the larger dispensational movement, prompting further study and dissemination of these apocalyptic concepts in North America.[5] Darby's timeline is strikingly like the one Scofield uses in the *Scofield Reference Bible*, though Scofield presents his dispensations as his and his alone without proper attribution, creating an amorphous mess of apocalyptic dispensational ideas. Darby was indeed a prominent figure of his era, but his work only achieved mainstream traction through Scofield because as Scofield's popularity grew, so too did Darby's, as people dug more into dispensational history to understand the how, why, and where of Scofield's argument.

Scofield practiced law before ministry and focused his fastidious and thorough attitude to understanding Christian Scripture to make something that missionaries and preachers could carry and use with ease. Thus, the *Scofield Reference Bible* was born and quickly became a gold standard of early 1900s American apocalypticism. Its popularity surprised even Scofield, which prompted him to revise and rerelease the study Bible in 1917 with an introduction explaining its intent and purpose:

> In the present edition, by a new system of connected topical references, all the greater truths of the divine revelation are so traced through the entire Bible, from the place of first mention to the last, that the reader may for himself follow the gradual unfolding of these, by many inspired writers through many ages, to their culmination in Jesus Christ and the New Testament Scriptures.[6]

Scofield—like Darby, Watts, and Edwards before him—sees the Bible as historically self-evident and believes that with guidance from someone "in the know" (in this case, Scofield) a layperson with little training can understand the current historical and political moment as it relates to biblical prophecy.

The publication of the *Scofield Reference Bible* was a watershed moment for dispensational apocalyptic thought, but Scofield presented his historical timeline in explicit terms years before in 1888 with the pamphlet *Rightly Dividing the Word of Truth*. He lays out seven historical theological dispensations in the pamphlet:

I. Man Innocent (before the Fall)
II. Man Under Conscience (after the Fall)
III. Man in Authority Over the Earth
    (Human Law)
IV. Man Under Promise (Abrahamic Covenant)
V. Man Under Law (From Moses to Jesus'
    Crucifixion)
VI. Man Under Grace (Jesus' Crucifixion to the
    Second Coming)
VII. Man Under the Personal Reign of Christ
    (Millennium Rule of Jesus Christ)[7]

Scofield's timeline is very similar to Watts' and Darby's respective apocalyptic calendars, so much that one must study each side by side to notice subtle differences. Each man claims something revelatory or unique, but these ideas simply reiterate something someone else already made as each makes Daniel and Revelation fit their circumstances without changing any interpretive content. Similarities and poor attribution aside, an important element of these four dispensation timelines is that each reconstructs history to situate itself near its end; the authors may claim to speak and write objectively, but the consistency of their respective conclusions says otherwise. Each writer resumes where others leave off, sees that the final dispensation has yet to begin, and declares his words as truth. American evangelical voices would continue to refine this tactic with conspicuous uniformity by situating their generation as the final one, meant to usher in Jesus' apocalyptic return. This means that Graham not only would have a historically contextual interpretive foundation to stand on; he also would have a full hermeneutical house to move into and in which to construct an outlet to amplify his voice.

From World War I to the Aftermath of World War II

World War I sent the United States and Europe into an existential spiral that only fanned the flames of dispensational apocalyptic thought. Promises of progress and prosperity disappeared following twenty million deaths and over twenty million wounded soldiers, prompting many Americans to ask, "Why?" and "How could this have happened?" Despite so many deaths, America's wartime victory overshadowed these losses as the economy boomed in the immediate postwar 1920s for much of white America, leading to an explosion of population and urbanization. The setting was ripe for young, dynamic ministers like George Truett, Harold Ockenga, John Rice, and William Riley to take the apocalyptic reins, which they did with great flair and vigor. They each took the existential dread following the sizeable loss of life and wed it to the nation's monetary success through large, carnival-like rallies and fiery radio broadcasts. Graham built his apocalyptic legacy upon their work; comparing these four preachers shows marked consistencies that would become staples of Graham's apocalyptic approach.

George Truett (1867–1944) preached "Baptists and Religious Liberty" on the East Steps of the National Capitol at Washington, D.C., on Sunday, May 16, 1920. The sermon adds a wrinkle to dispensationalist apocalyptic thought. Like Edwards, Watts, Darby, and Scofield, Truett believes his time is *the* time in which Jesus will return. However, unlike his dispensationalist forefathers, Truett believes the world will crumble if America remains isolationist. He argues that America turned the tide in Europe and WWI, cementing its place as God's chosen nation. Cutting other nations off will only allow the world to descend into madness, as its moral compass, America, stood by doing nothing.

Truett is indeed an unapologetic internationalist, but this international flavor comes at a price: he believes America represents God's will on earth and that other nations should follow America's path to success. Truett also carries harsh anti-Catholic sentiment, with his sermon sounding the alarm on America turning into a papal state. Without even realizing it, Truett echoes Luther's anti-Catholic position when he claims that individuals and nations should make their "own direct and immediate response to God," as he sees Catholicism as a pressing threat to American sovereignty.[8] Truett's fears likely arose from nationalized racism, spurred on by an influx of Italian Catholics in the late nineteenth and early twentieth centuries as they fled Italy's stifling rural poverty—a move that other evangelicals, including Graham, would continue by harboring disdain toward American Catholicism.[9]

Despite baseless apprehension about a hypothetical Catholic state, Truett spends much of the sermon urging the United States to take part in the newly formed League of Nations to protect American, and in turn global, interests. Truett also urges all citizens, including and especially elected officials, to heed his words:

> The people, all the people, are inexorably responsible for the laws, the ideals, and the spirit that are necessary for the

making of a great and enduring civilization. Every man of us is to remember that it is righteousness that exalteth a nation, and that it is sin that reproaches and destroys a nation.[10]

He follows this call for a righteous nation filled with righteous individuals by comparing America's status in the world to that of the good Samaritan: without America, the world would suffer and die like the man beaten and bruised in that parable's ditch. But just as the world needs America and its democratic government, so too does America need proper guidance:

> [America] needs Christ. He is the light of the world, nor is there any other sufficient light for the world. He is the solution of the world's complex questions, the one adequate Helper for its dire needs, the one only sufficient Saviour for our sinning race.[11]

Truett's logic here is straightforward: the world needs America to be a Christian nation so that the world may not perish but instead may have economic and spiritual wealth. He closes the address with words that could have come from Graham himself:

> Standing here today in the shadow of our country's Capitol, compassed about as we are with so great a cloud of witnesses, let us today renew our pledge to God, and to one another, that we will give our best to church and to state, to God and to humanity, by his grace and power, until we fall on the last sleep.[12]

Truett imbues his sermon with American divine power and positions himself as someone claiming to fight for democracy. He urges his listeners to be Christian but not Catholic, to fear government control unless it comes from "proper" Christians (that is, like Truett), and to reject overreaching ideologies save for the one that stresses America as the world's savior.

Truett's nationalistic sentiments echoed beyond that sermon into the larger evangelical discourse, and Harold John Ockenga (1905–1985) picked up where Truett left off. Graham and Ockenga share many connections, so much so that some scholars label the pair as the collective foundation for America's evangelical rebirth.[13] A key facet of this alleged evangelical revival is a renewed sense of American exceptionalism following World War II that preachers like Graham, Ockenga, and John Rice (1895–1980) built upon. It sparked when Mussolini invaded Ethiopia in 1935 and spun American evangelical apocalyptic fervor into a whirlwind, with Ockenga telling his American audience that humanity stood "on the brink of the greatest international upheaval and tribulation of history which will mark the end of the present era."[14] Ockenga's words ring with dispensationalist vigor when he describes this invasion as "the end of the present era," a marked difference from saying "the end of the world" or "end of existence." Ockenga stokes fear about the Italian encroachment to describe what is needed to protect American interests, a move that reflects his dispensationalist influence tied to American exceptionalism.

Like his explicit call to action regarding Mussolini's aggression on the African continent, Ockenga spoke openly about America's apocalyptic primacy early and often. For example, in his 1939 sermon "God Save America," Ockenga makes American exceptionalism a global theological priority: "Is America to be the last stand of civilization, a repository for Western civilization? Are we alone to emerge from this holocaust able to meet world communism unafraid? Are we then fulfilling our Divine mission?"[15] According to this message, the world and, in turn, God needs America to act and save it through prayer and personal salvation. Such overtly nationalistic theology reflects America's foreign policy at the time, as the nation saw Hitler, Mussolini, and Japan waging war but stood idle until Japan attacked Pearl Harbor in 1941. Thus, the type of salvation and preparation that Ockenga calls for is spiritual and not literal, or metaphorical and not physical, as his top priority is America's ability to foster an environment ripe for Christian salvation. It is worth noting that in this sermon, Ockenga also makes the false equivocation between the future Axis powers and communism, claiming that "world communism" is the most pressing threat to America and God's sovereignty despite an amicable relationship between the capitalist United States and the communist Soviet Union. As World War II escalated and the uneasy truce between the United States and the USSR became the backbone of the Allied powers, anticommunist rhetoric dwindled and waited like a fire seeking oxygen for Graham to step in and revive America's sense of destiny tied to free-market capitalism.

Rice followed a similar American exceptionalist vein, but, unlike Ockenga, he was openly biblical with his approach to World War II. Rice preached a sermon in 1935 titled "Is Mussolini the Anti-Christ?" with this subheading: "Will the Italio-Ethiopian War Reveal the Man of Sin and Re-establish The Roman Emipre [*sic*] as Foretold in the Bible? Should We Expect that Second Coming of Christ This Year?"[16] Here Rice takes Mussolini's surge as an attempt to reconstruct the Roman Empire, and he supports his claims with verses from Daniel, Revelation, and other prophetic books. In so doing, Rice continues the trend of so many previous Christian leaders in shaping his interpretation to fit his understanding of the global political structure without making America culpable for any part of the worldwide conflicts. This is a common trend among white evangelical leaders of the pre-WWII era, as they ignore financial and vocal support for Hitler and Mussolini from Americans like Henry Ford or Thomas Watson of IBM, which allowed fascist terror to reign for over a decade throughout Europe before American intervention. Their focus lies in presenting America as the bastion of Christian moral superiority that the world can imitate to ensure cosmic apocalyptic stability.

Rice's and Ockenga's ideas echo throughout Graham's life and work, but William Bell Riley (1861–1947) is perhaps the most direct line between evangelicals that preceded Graham and Graham's apocalyptic thought. Graham and Riley were very close, with Riley acting as a mentor of sorts for the young evangelist.

Riley groomed Graham as his eventual hand-picked replacement to succeed Riley as president of the Northwestern Bible School, a Bible college in Minnesota. Graham did serve as the school's president from 1948 to 1952 but left that role once popularity enabled him to preach and teach without additional employment. Riley was an outspoken Christian Fundamentalist who fought zealously against teaching evolution in public and private academic settings, a concern he coupled to an apocalyptic yoke when preaching about Christ's second coming.

Dispensationalist language soaks Riley's work. He often speaks of the coming millennium, Christ's imminent return, and the ticking clock of history present in Daniel and Revelation. He assails other dispensationalists that teach about a "wide gap" between the present moment and Jesus' return, saying that such placidity opposes Scripture and the urgent need to prepare as many people as one can.[17] In what eventually would become a staple of American evangelical apocalyptic rhetoric, Riley openly opposed Marxism and communism. He addresses these economic movements as certain apocalyptic evil:

> The seed of the righteous, not the proletariat, "shall inherit the earth" (Ps. 25:13). "Blessed are the meek," not labor unions, "for they shall inherit the earth" (Matt 5:5). The time of loyal subjection (every knee bowing in recognition of His authority, and every tongue confessing to His praise) will also be the period of righteous administration of government.[18]

Riley believes that human governments are fallible and flawed and that anyone promising utopia would only lead people astray. He does, however, believe that God would hand creation over to persons that remain faithful, citing Revelation for support. He also reads Daniel 2 as an allegory explaining what Riley saw as government decay at the hands of non-Christian leadership. Riley mocks President Woodrow Wilson's claim that World War I was "the world's last; a war to end all war" by saying, "Such an explanation, of course, was essential in modernist philosophy and could be harmonized with the evolutionary theory."[19] Riley argues that to the corrupted mind, the rot and deterioration shown in Daniel 2 looks like progress. Minds like Riley claim that they know better when they see through the lies of so-called progressive human improvement. Fallout from WWI that lead to WWII sparked Riley into apocalyptic interpretive action. He argues that a global consolidation of power is a clear step toward fulfilling prophecies of Armageddon in Daniel and Revelation, interpreting the ten horns of Revelation 17:12 as the roadmap for what will happen when small nations work together and collaborate for peace:

> A few years ago the kingdoms and nations of the earth required three figures for their enumeration, but now the little nations are being fast wiped out of existence; their potentates stripped of all power and, in the case of China—the world's largest nation—is threatened at least with absorption. In other words, it begins to see how quickly the true potentates of the earth might be reduced to the small number of ten: prophecies that have appeared so impossible of fulfillment are rapidly being displaced by history that parallels their very existence.[20]

He describes the swirling winds of another looming war as divinely controlled judgement, saying that God holds Satan on a leash that allows Satan to do only what God wants. This is indeed the end times for Riley, and he warns not to ward off the blows of tyranny and fascism through action. Rather, he wants more people to become Christian and profess their faith so that when Jesus comes they would leave the fallen world behind. Thus, Riley speaks directly about the seeds of World War II to weave the future Axis powers into his apocalyptic eschatology:

> When Japan makes up its mind to attack China, and Hitler his mind to attack every contiguous nation, and even some beyond channels and seas, and Mussolini to join hands in the mass murder, God consents, saying—"Loose the angels of war," if you will. Just as for the battle of Armageddon He will give the same command and permit the slaying of the third part of men.[21]

Riley's theology of war reveals a dangerous and selfish conceit: showing the shallow pride behind an American-centric lens, he believes that God blessed the war and the death of millions with divine permission. America's place here is to stoke the fires of war by letting them burn, as the only true path to salvation lies in claiming Jesus Christ as the nation's Lord and Savior and in making itself a nation under God's cosmic blessing.

Riley's nationalistic apocalypticism reflects a place of profound privilege and safety. Japan, China, Hitler, Mussolini, and other agents that he claims God loosed upon the world in righteous judgment never threatened his health and well-being. Riley never felt the war face to face, as the contiguous United States of America could sit back and watch the world tear itself apart, protected by the "confines" of the Atlantic and Pacific Oceans. He talked about what is happening rather than talking with the people who were fighting and dying, which is paradigmatic of Graham's theological orientation. As with Graham's early days, Riley was comfortable watching the world crumble around him without using his position and platform to sway opinions and save lives. This gets to the heart of evangelical apocalyptic theology, as the people talking about the world's dire state are so rarely directly involved.

This disconnect between the warfront and home front may explain why American citizens imbued the conflict between the Allied forces and Axis powers with great importance in terms of cultural mythology. World War II remains a seminal event in Western history, as its impact on evangelical apocalyptic continually shapes American political, social, and religious ideals. Known as the "Greatest Generation," Americans that fought and served the nation during the Second World War are credited by many scholars and laypersons with building the world's greatest economic superpower. Historical perspectives, however, remain bound by cultural orientation and ethnicity, as the victory and birth of the modern American nation-state carried the burden of it also being the first (and still only) nation to use nuclear weapons during wartime. Victory for American soldiers and workers also raised issues about local politics, as ideologies like discrimination and bigotry that so many fought to defeat thrived on American soil. African American soldiers helped defeat Nazi Germany, liberate Mussolini's Italy, and eliminate threats on the Pacific front, only to return home to Jim Crow segregation laws, financial restrictions, and educational limitations. Further, American women went from being vital to the wartime economic system to bystanders, prompting a sense of dissonance and dissatisfaction with the status quo. Dissension prompted grassroots movements, ultimately leading to the civil rights era and second-wave feminism of the 1950s and 1960s.[22]

Simmering social upheaval produced more anxiety when paired with a tool central to American success in World War II, one that prompted as much fear as it did certainty and comfort: the atomic bomb. American evangelical leaders saw the destructive capabilities that humanity now carried as a blessing *and* a curse because the weapons that produce peace now only do so on the back of much death. Evangelical pastors pounced on Hiroshima and Nagasaki, including and especially a twenty-seven-year-old Billy Graham. With the sermon "The Second Coming of Christ," he made his stance about nuclear force clear when he said he shouted "Hallelujah" in response to America's nuclear attack on Japan. However, Graham was not alone in his jubilant response to widespread death, as W. A. Criswell, a pastor and preacher peer of Graham's, expressed similar sentiments, even as he also viewed human progress as faulty, borderline idolatrous, and doomed to fail.

Criswell echoed Riley's disdain for social advancement and mocked improvements in automobiles, televisions, and refrigerators, claiming that no amount of human goodwill overtakes celestial evil:

> All right, my conclusion: there is not a vestigial remnant of evidence to be found in all history that good ever overtakes evil. The thing is in a cycle; and it is vicious, and it is terrible. It was evil in the days of Abraham. It was evil in the days of Isaiah. It was evil in the days of Jesus. It was evil in the days

of Paul. It was evil in the days of Charlemagne. It was evil in the days of Napoleon Bonaparte. It was evil in the days of Kaiser Wilhelm II. It was evil in the days of Hitler, and Tojo, and Mussolini; and it is evil today. And if the cycle continues to go as it has in days past, the hour will come when the whole world will be another Hiroshima—quailing, trembling before the lurid death that falls out of the sky.[23]

Hiroshima and Nagasaki are paradoxical events for Criswell, as he decries the human drive leading to the bomb's creation but looks upon its destruction as positive evidence supporting his apocalyptic claims. The question then becomes: What made Criswell become an important but minor evangelical figure compared to Graham's national and international success? How did Criswell affect Graham's message, and how did the relationship between the dueling evangelists set Graham on a path that led him to the Eisenhower White House?

Graham's Rival: W. A. Criswell and His Apocalyptic Worldview

Upon Criswell's death in 2002, President George W. Bush and First Lady Laura Bush released a statement: "Dr. Criswell was an important spiritual leader for America. He was a man of deep and abiding faith who brought comfort to the thousands who heard his message of hope, love and compassion." The president's words reflect the wider influence of Criswell and his work, which began officially when he took his first pastorate at First Baptist Church of Chickasha, Oklahoma, in 1937. He served Chickasha until taking another pastorate in Muskogee, Oklahoma, from 1941 to 1944, a move that pivoted him toward the pastorate that launched his national career in 1944 with First Baptist Church in Dallas. George Truett rocketed FBC Dallas toward notoriety, but Criswell moved the church to greater heights, as membership increased to over twenty-nine thousand people during his fifty-year pastoral tenure. Criswell and Graham shared similar theological sentiments, as they read Scripture as infallible and inerrant, saw imminent cosmic danger threatening human existence, argued that widespread Christian revival would cure all evils, and presented America and its interests as a salve for fallen humanity. However, unlike Graham, Criswell articulated his positions with sharper and more contentious rhetoric, which may explain why Graham became a beloved international figure over Criswell. Brazen in opposing the separation of church and state, Criswell once argued that church-state separation was created by "some infidel's imagination" for the benefit of Christianity's enemies.[24] Digging deeper into Criswell's church-and-state position shows that it stems from Criswell's hardline anti-Catholic views, and the separation he wanted was between a papal state and America becoming a "true" (non-Catholic) Christian nation. Criswell also harbored dissatisfaction with America, despite its considerable economic success following World War II, and he saw the nation teetering on the edge of destruction. He blamed perceived American instability on an unsubstantiated claim that "more than ten thousand soothsayers, necromancers, fortunetellers, swamis" had infiltrated the American government, declaring that the situation echoed the world of Daniel when "Babylon, where Daniel lived, was the headquarters of the soothsayers and the necromancers in the ancient day."[25] Criswell's tactic here is bizarre, as the "evidence" he used to support this "soothsayer" claim is nothing more than his reflections regarding cultural and political changes. Yet that did not stop him from tossing blame around without reproach, nor did it stop him from making claims about unseen supernatural forces controlling America behind the scenes.

Language of "fortunetellers" and "swamis" shows one piece to the puzzle of why Criswell never achieved Graham's level of notoriety. Another is that Criswell began his political machinations later than Graham, beginning in earnest during a 1980 national religious roundtable in which Criswell prayed and Ronald Reagan stumped for reelection. Criswell and Reagan's connections continued and became more public at the 1984 Republican National Convention where Criswell prayed, thanking God for Reagan's renomination. Criswell's preaching and teaching left visible marks on U.S. history through his relationship with Reagan and other political figures, granting them avenues to express pro-American theological stances under the guise of "America First" politics. However, unlike Graham, Criswell's rhetorical presence lacked broader presence and influence, likely due to Criswell's strict and vitriolic readings of Daniel and Revelation. Both Graham and Criswell preached similar apocalyptic messages, but how Criswell presented his apocalypticism makes him seem more radical while also making Graham seem tamer and warmer.

In the spirit of a more aggressive stance, Criswell called out what he sees as American ills early and often in his career. On December 31, 1944, on the cusp of a new year, he urged leaders to turn the nation back to God:

> What if our Commander in Chief, and our general staff, our legislators, our senators, our representatives of our people, what if they were to turn to God and say, "O God, we can't rule without Thee, we can't govern without Thee. Thou must be our great Commander in Chief. We yield this leadership unto Thee."[26]

Similarly, in other sermons, Criswell berated the Internal Revenue Service and claimed they favored the Catholic Church. He decried this destructive Catholic bias and argued that it blurs the lines between church and state, while still in other sermons he urged leaders and hearers to bring the country back to God.[27] Thus, for Criswell, American Catholicism represents a direct threat to "true" American Christianity and, in turn, national sovereignty. He rails against prayer being taken out of schools and cited specific examples from Dallas County, Texas. Criswell sees prayer woven into America's soul and believes that removing explicit references to God went against the nation's very fabric:

> What has happened to America, when it is unacceptable and out of place to name the name of God, even in the presence of our children at a commencement exercise of a public high

school? Something has happened to the soul, and the heart, and the life of America, and something is going to happen to the destiny of our people, except we turn.[28]

Such staunch opposition to anything beyond what Criswell deems right or correct makes one note that compared to Criswell's aggressive denouncing, Graham appears less driven by patriotism and more focused on pleasing God. Yet that is what makes Graham's apocalyptic rhetoric so effective, in that he could slip something as political as "If America falls, the divine structure falls" past viewers and readers with considerable ease. Criswell lacked delicacy in his language toward America and was not afraid to let his anti-Catholic stance drive his xenophobic theology home like a hammer to a nail. Conversely, while Graham also maintained a negative appraisal he used a softer touch to speak broadly about Catholicism and concerns for America's well-being.

Like Criswell's advice to America and its leadership, any pretense of subtlety in the association between Daniel and the Christian New Testament found in Graham's work disappears in Criswell's apocalyptic sermons. In "Daniel and Revelation," a sermon preached in 1968, Criswell lists direct connections between Daniel and the New Testament to argue that "the Book of Daniel was loved, studied, known, and quoted by our Saviour," followed by a list of comparisons between Daniel and Matthew.[29] Not mincing words, Criswell writes:

> Matthew 24:15 equals Daniel 9:27; 11:31; 12:11. Matthew 24:21 equals Daniel 12:1. Matthew 24:30 equals Daniel 7:13. Matthew 26:64 equals Daniel 7:13. John 5:28, 29 equal Daniel 12:2. Matthew 14:43 equals Daniel 12:3. All of these passages but emphasize the close study of the Book of our Lord Jesus Christ.[30]

Criswell expands his take on the relationship between Daniel and Revelation, saying (without evidence) that other New Testament authors like Paul, Peter, and the author of Hebrews made Daniel part of their "study and spiritual searching."[31] He concludes with a pointed and direct declaration that "whether we read of the kingdom of Daniel, or whether we read of the kingdom in the Revelation, both prophecies are the same."[32] These unequivocal readings and preaching set Criswell's reception paradigm apart from Graham, as Criswell declared and preached his particular doctrinal interpretations as opposed to personal or communal spiritual enrichment, a tactic that would grant Graham considerable political access.

Criswell continued reading Daniel and Revelation as sibling texts throughout his ministry. He uses one to justify the other in his 1972 sermon "The Beast Nations":

> And in that apocalyptic writing, Daniel has no peer except it be the apostle John, who wrote the Revelation. The comparison between those two apocalyptic writers is always interesting. Daniel is preeminently the prophet of the times of the Gentiles, and he follows the sweep of human history until the coming of Christ into His terrestrial, earthly supremacy. The apostle John presents the apocalyptic future, the sweep of history unto the coming of Christ into His celestial supremacy, when the heavens and the hosts of all creation are made subject to the King and Lord of all. Both men—both apocalyptic writers by symbol, by picture, they present the whole story of human history until the great consummation of the conquering, coming Christ.[33]

Here Criswell presses and reads Daniel as a gentile prophet positioned to illuminate Jesus' eventual arrival at the start of what Criswell calls Revelation's apocalyptic future. Daniel 2 becomes a prophetic portend to Christ, as Criswell ties Christianity's messianic figure to the "stone cut without hands" at Daniel 2:34:

> And when the revelation was revealed concerning the meaning, the ten toes were struck by the stone cut without hands—and that was the coming of Christ and the establishment of His millennial kingdom. So in the second chapter of the Book of Daniel, that image of the great man, we have followed the course of history to the coming of Christ.[34]

Criswell preaches Daniel and Revelation as profoundly Christian and reads the two apocalyptic texts as presenting a history that will culminate in Christ's terrestrial and celestial supremacy over human governments, without sacrificing America's "special" place in the divine order.

Graham and Criswell knew each other well, and both worked American evangelist circuits and benefited greatly from increased religious zeal following World War II. The pair formed a tight bond over many years, with Criswell tracing their relationship's roots to 1953 and the day when Graham became of member of Criswell's very own First Baptist Church of Dallas. Criswell described it in almost sacred terms:

> William Randolph Hearst in California, played up the great crusade that Billy Graham was holding in Los Angeles. So when the hour came for him to hold the revival meeting in our dear church, you couldn't begin to start to commence to accommodate the people. So we took Billy Graham to the Cotton Bowl, and he held the revival meeting, the crusade, in the Cotton Bowl: one of the tremendous beginning ministries of this century. And best of all and sweetest of all and dearest of all, in that crusade, on Sunday morning, down the aisle came Billy Graham and joined. And I have been his pastor ever since.[35]

Graham's recollection of joining this church resembles Criswell's account in that both stories end with Graham joining First Baptist Church in Dallas. Graham spurned Criswell's grandiose statements about that day marking some great cosmic significance, with his biographer William Martin quoting Graham to indicate this divide:

> His reason for maintaining membership in a church so far from his home in Montreat was disarmingly simple: "If I belonged to a Baptist church in the neighborhood, they would continually be asking me to work in church affairs. When I'm at home I attend my wife's Presbyterian church and naturally they don't ask me to do anything."[36]

Comparing Criswell and Graham's respective stories about one event does not suggest animosity or misrepresentation by either. It indicates, rather, that despite significant cultural and political impact, Criswell's sentiment toward Graham reflects mild inferiority, which explains why Criswell's retelling of Graham's church membership conflicts with Graham's matter-of-fact pragmatism.

Yet one aspect of Criswell's and Graham's respective work with Daniel and Revelation bears striking consistency: though they differ in terms of expressing overt anti-Catholic jingoism, their receptions teem with American exceptionalism. The United States of America and what Graham and Criswell call "American Democracy" dominate their apocalyptic writings and teachings. Both claim the fall of America will yield global destruction culminating in events foretold in Scripture. Their respective ties between America and how they interpret Scripture would make many Americans eager to follow their lead, as Graham and Criswell attracted American citizens with certain patriotic zeal. Both evangelists experienced swelling popularity due to their biblical patriotism, and both worked hard to cement their public theo-political personas. For Graham especially, this popularity made political strategists notice potential voters in crowds attending evangelical rallies and sermons. It is through such notoriety that Graham tapped executive political power through presidential relationships, beginning with Eisenhower. Conversely, it was not until Reagan's presidential election that Criswell gained political capital. Criswell's political aspirations came too late.

In Graham's Hands

A discussion of the people that preceded and influenced Graham produces an effect much like a broken record. One evangelist after another preached and taught about impending global threats like communism, war, and secular law to ground their apocalyptic worldview in Scripture. Graham's "Now is the time!" and "If America falls, the world falls!" messages indeed built upon what many prominent Christians that came before had said. So the question is this: What made Graham's worldview stick? What about him compelled Eisenhower and many other U.S. presidents to grant Graham access to international power? Graham's intentional openness paired with a strict doctrinal understanding of America's place in the global landscape is the most probable answer. Graham—unlike Criswell, Riley, Rice, Ockenga, Scofield, Darby, Watts, and Edwards—encouraged his listeners to be a part of something great and rewarding, to join in the celestial celebration that God lays out for nations that openly declare their faith. Conversely, Graham's apocalyptic thought rang with echoes of more rigid interpretations, as he never dropped the "or else" mindset, which he used to his advantage as he wove his thought into the streams of power that would produce the pledge.

THREE

BILLY GRAHAM'S APOCALYPTIC WORLDVIEW

As Graham aged, his public persona grew cuddlier and warmer, making him into America's sweet evangelical grandfather. Upon Graham's death in 2018, the *New York Times* published a piece praising Graham's ability to reach across the political aisle. The paper declared, "America's preacher has left us, and we need him now more than ever."[1] Publishers ran his name on books in self-help and Christian-living sections with images of Graham smiling warmly across brightly colored glossy covers. These books linked Graham's personal insights with his understandings of grace, forgiveness, and individual piety, becoming tracts about living well with hints of his early evangelical zeal.

Age also brought milder and kinder sermons as his political and social positions softened to something far more generalized than the "America first" mindset of Graham's early years. In a 2006 sermon, "The Love of God," given in Baltimore, Graham opened with deliberate calm:

> We are living in a world of great turmoil and confusion. I
> do not recall in my lifetime since World War II that there's
> been a moment like this, maybe never before have we been
> threatened as we are being threatened today. And some peo-
> ple are even predicting that we are heading toward a nuclear
> war, which would be something far beyond imagination. I
> was at Hiroshima just after the Japanese war. I will never
> forget that they wouldn't let you go near certain areas and
> also in North Korea, we went to North Korea . . . and if ever
> a place needs prayer, it's there.[2]

Graham's sympathetic words here differ wildly from sermons and radio discussions in which he celebrates bombing Hiroshima and Nagasaki with a confident and righteous "Hallelujah."[3] Such a statement likely would shock and embarrass the older and wiser evangelist, and comparing the elder Graham's compassion to the younger Graham's vitriol shows that the man he became does not resemble who he then was. However, investigating Graham's actual interpretive work shows that, even as he aged, Graham never shook this American-centric rhetoric. Instead, he simply made the language more palatable by adapting it to fit shifting historical and cultural currents.

This chapter—by analyzing books, sermons, and interviews— examines the aging Graham's language adjustments in detail, specifically how Graham accommodated societal changes without losing his trademark American apocalyptic exceptionalism. Said analysis shows that Graham's interpretations of Daniel and Revelation were major factors in his life and ministry that sparked his ongoing political involvement, culminating in his push to legislate "under God" into the Pledge of Allegiance. The first step here is to show how Graham read Daniel and Revela-tion as a singular window into America's future, creating space for him to argue that if listeners ignore his words, then death and destruction will be the nation's and, in turn, the world's ulti-mate destination. Step two shows that Graham believed Daniel and Revelation told him that if America simply says it belongs to God, then God will protect and bless the nation by saving it from certain doom. Graham's "make America godly again" approach is standard evangelical fare, but what separates Graham from other evangelical voices is that he believes the seizure of power is God's ordained key to success and stability for the United States. Graham took this unapologetically political approach when he preached and taught about a national revival, urging his audience to "cry out" for God's help and to submit themselves to God. From Graham's perspective and according to his apocalyptic view, Americans' pledge of divine allegiance is a crucial first step toward ensuring stability: economic, military, social, political, and cultural.

Graham's Rise after World War II: 1945–1955

Words licked like fiery tongues as Graham preached "Why God Allows Communism to Flourish" to thousands in a 1949 rally in Los Angeles. The first ten minutes crescendo to questions like "Why do the righteous suffer?" or "Why does God allow good Christian people to be persecuted?" and "Why doesn't God stop all the pestilence and all the famine and all the war and all the suffering and all the sin and end it all?"[4] The sermon climaxes with Graham declaring that God will one day end all evil things, including shutting down "the liquor houses," in accordance with Graham's understanding of Revelation through the return of Jesus sounded by the archangel. Such would herald the beginning of a glorious thousand-year reign. Graham builds upon the sermon's Revelation imagery with a diatribe against worldly powers, saying that "Joe Stalin thinks he can run the world" and "the UN thinks they can run the world," and culminating with "Jesus is gonna step in one of these days and show 'em how the world oughta be run" as his audience responds with cheers, shouts, and clapping affirmation.[5] "God," Graham says with confidence, "is the only one that has the world's solutions."[6] Soviet communism, which Graham defines as "the fanatical religion that has declared war on God himself," is his and, therefore, the world's greatest foe. Graham weaves this tapestry of American-centric God-praising alongside Soviet-bashing to issue a bold proclamation: Soviet communism is the vehicle through which God will bring about the final battle of Armageddon, which Graham declares will make Germany's defeat in 1945 pale in comparison.[7]

The sermon lasts over forty-five minutes, and throughout its first half Graham moves between pointed political apocalyptic rhetoric and traditional "convert or suffer eternally in hell" evangelical discussion points. Yet political rhetoric overpowers Graham's Christian repentance language when he connects apocalyptic imagery from Matthew 24 to struggles between communist and capitalist nations. He paraphrases the verses while providing personal commentary:

> Now listen, now listen to this, and ye shall hear of wars and rumors of wars for nation shall rise against nation and kingdom against kingdom. I was told that the interpretation of that passage of Scripture means kingdoms against kingdoms, now that means world alliances, that means an eastern bloc or a western bloc, that means the allies against the central powers. Kingdoms against kingdoms and in this century we've had two world wars within the last thirty years. Two world wars, in the last thirty years, fulfilling the prophecy of Jesus Christ 1900 years ago! I wanna tell ya, the third World War is going to make the others look like a little fistfight compared to the other World War that could come in the next five years unless Christ comes.[8]

Graham implores his Los Angeles audience to repent of their sins, or else they (and the world) will suffer the consequences of Graham's announced World War III. Graham believes and preaches a contingent apocalyptic perspective: the physical world threatens itself and the people in it, but God can prevent all bad things about to happen if Americans turn from their sins and accept Jesus as their personal and thereby political savior. This early sermon presents a foundational tenet to Graham's apocalyptic worldview, as the threat of Soviet communism drove and motivated much of his early ministry. It also shows how seamlessly Graham continued the Christian tradition of molding apocalyptic interpretation to fit one's historical context. According to Graham, Daniel and Revelation speak directly to *his* circumstances; to read otherwise is to endanger preacher and audience.

Graham returned often to themes of apocalyptic dread in those same 1949 Los Angeles sermon rallies. For example, he opens the sermon "Final Judgment" by discussing a conversation between himself and a listener expressing gratitude for Graham's ability to preach and teach effectively and easily. The man, whom Graham describes as a "minister of one of the largest churches in town," asks Graham, "Please don't emphasize judgment so much; why don't you preach on love a little more? Have more pathos in your messages, and I don't believe you oughta preach judgment so much."[9] Graham shares his distraught and saddened response to the crowds, saying he cried out to God after the conversation and begged for forgiveness in case emphasizing divine judgement was incorrect. Graham then responds to himself, as his next words make clear that he believes the minister's trepidation was not only wrong but also dangerous: "I believe we are living in the last moment of history, I believe time's final drama is about to be enacted, and I believe we are living at the very last days."[10] Los Angeles–area churches then draw Graham's ire when he declares that "lukewarm" belief leaves America susceptible to ungodly influences like communism and that people avoiding sermons about divine judgment put themselves, their congregation, and their nation at risk.

He claims that because of this conversation with an unnamed pastor, Graham recommits himself to sharing this apocalyptic message, which he constructs through reading Daniel and Revelation as apocalyptic prophecies geared toward American audiences.[11] Doing anything less than that only sets Americans on a path toward destruction. Graham makes the United States both the benefactor of divine mercy and the vehicle through which God's destruction affects the entire world: if America follows God, the world will thrive, but when America does not, the world faces destruction. Despite his fervor, at times Graham backtracks, saying things like Christians are "strangers in this land" and "I am not a citizen of America . . . I am in one sense but I am a citizen of God."[12] He quickly returns, however, to communism as the global catalyst for destruction: "When the communists get here, we're gonna find out who is who."[13] God will soon usher faithful believers "to the marriage supper of the lamb," meaning that Graham identifies this communist threat as the wicked evil foretold in Daniel and Revelation that will help God decide who is worth saving and who is not.[14]

In another sermon from the same 1949 Los Angeles gathering, titled "The Second Coming of Christ," the topic soon turns to nuclear weapon capacity and military proliferation. Graham cites data from Robert Maynard Hutchins, then chancellor of the University of Chicago, to offer a celestial compare-and-contrast: "There are enough atomic bombs in the American stockpile that if they all were exploded at once, it would burn the whole world up. Well if man can do that, what more can God do with his atomic energy when he comes?"[15] Graham then creates a general but America-focused apocalyptic timeline by arguing that regardless of when Jesus will return, people will always be unprepared. He emphasizes this perspective, saying that "almost every reference to the second coming of Jesus Christ is linked to a practical exhortation," as merely believing in a second coming is insufficient without proper outward and visible response.[16] To Graham, one must prove one's faith with an outward and vocal expression.

He then makes his message personal as he asks the audience, "Did you know that the second coming is what lead me to Jesus Christ? . . . My mother was born again and led to Christ by studying the second coming of Christ" (despite what he describes as encouragement from her local pastor to avoid studying John's Apocalypse).[17] Graham uses his mother's conversion to argue that anyone focused too much on knowing or deciphering exact dates and identities misses the point of Revelation, only to make a hard pivot and claim that the nation of Israel's existence and the rise of Soviet Russia underscore Jesus' imminent return. He emphasizes this point continually: "I believe we are living in events unprecedented in this history of the world . . . events predicted in Daniel, predicted in Revelation, that are predicted throughout the Scriptures."[18] Graham uses Daniel 12:4 (and the line "many shall run to and fro, and knowledge shall be increased") as proof that the proliferation of knowledge, expanded literacy, and expedited travel through airplanes and trains portends Jesus' return.[19] Such language shows that to Graham unrestricted social progress and growth brings doom while America is the bastion holding back the flames of Armageddon.

The message takes a shocking turn when he describes his reaction to America's bombing of Hiroshima and Nagasaki:

> When that atomic bomb exploded off Hiroshima, I was sorry for those poor people but in one sense of the word, I said, "Hallelujah! it's a sign that the end is about here!" Because in the first time for the history of the world man has in his hands weapons to destroy himself with and that's exactly what God said in his word.[20]

Praising the destruction of over one hundred thousand lives is unsettling and disturbing but also quintessentially evangelical and accords with Graham's apocalyptic rhetoric. Such wanton death and destruction only fuel the flames of end times, and, where many react with horror, evangelical Christians bask in the glow of what they hope will come. He concludes with more fearmongering over communism, saying that Soviet communists will invade and "hang all of us on the same tree" unless America repents and turns to God.[21] Such is the apocalyptic interpretive pattern Graham mimics: catastrophic events happen to other people and places, but they *must* happen to usher in the great peace Jesus' return will bring. Only those who properly acknowledge God will be spared from the coming doom.

In the next decade, Graham's apocalyptic mindset crystalized around ideas broached at the 1949 Los Angeles rally. For example, the sermon titled "War and Peace" (1950) discusses the escalating Korean conflict as proof for supernatural evil alongside calls for American repentance. In 1951, Graham speaks directly about political machinations and movements to urge his audience to pray aggressively for American leaders in Washington, D.C., claiming that unseen satanic powers run amok and threaten America's sovereignty by attacking its spiritual well-being. He summarizes his position succinctly: "The destiny of the world is vitally related to the survival of America. The downfall of America would be a great atrocity bringing repercussions on a global scale."[22] In 1952, Graham's rhetoric expands beyond divine inevitability to include historical possibility when he claims, "I believe if the American people had a great spiritual revival that judgments predicted in the Bible would not fall upon us."[23] This is a cause-and-effect shift in Graham's beliefs, as America still heads toward judgment of biblical proportions, but changing the country's spirituality can stall God's wrath.

The question then becomes one regarding specifics about what America needs to do and how it needs to do it to avoid divine reproach. Graham offers vague solutions alongside increased nationalism, saying that humans must care about divine and worldly leaders, invoking "render unto Caesar what is Caesar's" from Matthew 22:21. National sovereignty for the sake of national sovereignty, and not mere religious piety, became part of Graham's preaching repertoire as he prioritized American stability over and against non-American governments: anyone opposing America opposes God. Perhaps what is most peculiar about Graham's 1950s patriotism is his apparent self-contradiction: in sermons preached in 1949, Graham speaks of his earthly citizenship as a mere obligation, stressing that his true citizenship lies in heaven. However, in sermons like "America's Need for Spiritual Awakening," he claims the opposite should motivate American Christians:

> There are many Christians that I know that say we are not to be concerned about world affairs, that we are to take no

part in the things of this world because our citizenship in heaven. To take this attitude is to ignore the plain teachings of Scripture that a true Christian will be a good citizen and will be deeply concerned about his fellow man. . . . Christians should be in honest, fervent prayer that God might spare our nation.[24]

One could argue that Graham uses national sovereignty to bring people to Christ, but continually insisting on American preeminence coats the evangelist's fervor with narrow xenophobia that sanctifies doom and destruction.

Joseph Stalin's death in March 1953 sent shockwaves beyond Graham's purview, as newly elected president Eisenhower addressed Stalin's death that April, along with the release of American POWs during a United Nations–sponsored exchange at Pyongyang, North Korea. People around the world, including Graham, sat watching and waiting for Eisenhower's response, and Eisenhower gave them what became arguably his most prominent public address with "The Chance for Peace." In the address, later called the "Cross of Iron" speech, Eisenhower presents his ideology of peace woven with calls for increasing nuclear armament. Eisenhower addresses the imminent need to fight Russia with nonmilitary means like improving America's "roads and schools, hospitals and homes, food, and health."[25] However, Eisenhower does not soften his militaristic stance, as his message embodies a "both-and" approach: infrastructure and global trust come in addition to American military power, making it clear that America will not yield its position of strength. Captivated, Graham anoints Eisenhower his "chosen one," as the president says that his proposed domestic and foreign policies "conform to our firm faith that God created man to enjoy, not destroy, the fruits of the earth and of their own toil."[26]

Eisenhower's language fueled patriotic zeal across the nation, which Graham used as an opportunity. Graham preached that Revelation and Daniel presented Soviet communism as the antichrist and that American Christianity was the world's messiah. Communism came from Satan himself in the form of economic repentance that promised a new world and utopian way of life, only to lead people into destruction. The unambiguously titled April 1953 sermon, "Mr. President," given soon after "The Chance for Peace," actively exhibits American messianism: there, Graham puts his American-centric apocalyptic Christianity on full display and eliminates any possible equivocation, saying to Eisenhower, "We hold that the only ultimate answer to communism is Christianity."[27]

Graham's Rise to National and International Prominence: 1954–1965

In 1954, Eisenhower added "under God" to the Pledge of Allegiance, stoking Graham's American apocalyptic passions. The president moved one step toward the America that Graham believed God wanted. Graham preached that year aboard the SS *United States* cruise liner. In his address, he notes that the ship can proudly ferry fourteen thousand troops into an active warzone should the need arise. Graham presents the boat's destination, Great Britain, as an unchurched and unreligious land, calling Americans to lend fervent prayer on his travels to missionize and proselytize. He praises and motivates his listeners on their profoundly American journey and Christian purpose:

> As we stand on board the ship and look back to the shores of America over two-thousand miles away we cannot help thanking God that we're Americans. We look at America as greatly blessed of God. While millions in other lands will go to bed hungry tonight, most Americans will sleep on a full stomach. Other nations are on the verge of financial bankruptcy and are have difficulty with keeping the wolf of financial collapse away from their national doors.[28]

Graham pivots and references Luke 19 and Matthew 23, when Jesus weeps for Jerusalem, to argue that Jerusalem's first-century fall at the hands of Rome came from Jerusalem rejecting Jesus. He then implores his American audience to change, saying it is their "righteous duty and patriotic obligation" to heed that warning, repent as a nation, or suffer Jerusalem's fate.[29] China and their communist revolution prove the consequences of America's "spiritual complacency," as Graham says, "We lost China seven years ago because American foreign policy wasn't founded on moral principle."[30] In short, China fell because America fell. Graham believes that American–Chinese relations falter thanks to theological inconsistency. Solutions lie not in doctrine or diplomacy; rather, "the only hope for our nation is faith in Jesus Christ. . . . Americans must be born again; our nation is inseparably linked with Jesus Christ."[31]

Apocalyptic worldview on high alert, Graham went on to preach in New Orleans about "certain small atheistic groups" working to eliminate "In God We Trust" from American coinage.[32] These unnamed atheistic groups apparently presented a grave and imminent threat to Graham, requiring an active response. Graham describes America's "corporate faith in God" via public professions of faith like "In God We Trust" as the secret to all of America's success, and removing this statement "would be a signal that we no longer trust in almighty God."[33] America's cataclysmic end becomes the most probable outcome, with Graham exclaiming, "If you will take your Bible in one hand and your history book in the other, and use your God-given intellect you will conclude that no nation ever has, can now, or ever will long endure unless it acknowledges that inevitable divine rule."[34] Millions of American Christians and active churches mean little compared to public professions of faith, as what the world sees as America's standards are what God uses as a measuring stick for global destruction.

Graham's weekly *Hour of Decision* radio show flourished and granted him opportunities to preach and teach across the nation and around the world with minimal travel; radio waves took him anywhere he wanted. The show also exposed international audiences to his apocalyptic mindset, giving him almost universal reach. Graham used the show to nuance certain teachings and ideas, but continually he returned to what he called America's dangerous "surface" interest in religion. For example, in the broadcast "Christ Is Coming" (1955), Graham declares that "surface interest in religion will not suffice, ye must be born again!"[35] Further, in "Are These the End Times?" (1956), Graham answers his own question with a resounding affirmation: Russian troop movement in Eastern Europe and growing Chinese economic power only signal Armageddon. Scripture speaks plainly and truly about current events; individuals without expressed Christian faith will not survive. Here his apocalyptic position appears at odds with itself, as Graham stresses America's allegiance to God as an apocalyptic salve. However, in the same sermon he makes political intrigue inevitable; the only way to stop the end is to prevent it through faith in Jesus.

Themes of America's fate tied to religiosity are common in Graham's preaching, but Graham began tying American sovereignty to world peace as the 1950s progressed and Cold War tensions grew. In "Our Nation Must Repent," Graham argues that America stands against communism like Elijah protecting Israel. He claims that it takes "one man, one nation, standing alone with dog-less faith, facing an entire army" to earn victory and that "only a humbled, repentant nation with faith and trust in almighty God can possibly win the battle against communism."[36] The sermon concludes with a desperate plea for patriotic religious declaration: "If God sees no repentance, we will be as Sodom and Gomorrah. . . . I beg of you, I implore of you that if you love the Stars and Stripes, if you have any patriotism in your soul, that you as an American will give heed to the Word of God."[37]

The last two years of the 1950s brought increased anxiety for Graham, as his messages on the apocalypse and end times increased and his rhetoric intensified, but details become inexact. For example, in "The Handwriting on the Wall" (1958), Graham declares that an ambiguous and nondescript "crisis" consumes America. He preaches about Daniel 5 and ties Belshazzar's death to Americans being in the world but not of the world: "The time to return to a national faith has come" as God judges America because its citizens "commit every sin known to the world . . . and have been found wanting."[38] He closes with assurance that "the most patriotic thing you can do this night is to give your life to Jesus Christ."[39] Russia remains America's and therefore the world's foremost threat. Succumbing to the evils of communism and materialism (an unlikely pairing) is an inevitability, as Graham's cry for national salvation remains profoundly apocalyptic: the end is indeed coming, Russia and the political climate prove it, and hell awaits if America stays unprepared.[40]

Sermons received more assertive titles in the early 1960s, like "Prepare for the Storm," "God Bless America," and "Climax of History." Graham preached in more "exotic" locales, including Israel, Paraguay, and Brazil. His rhetoric, however, synchronized with apocalyptic warnings that communal instability would become a threat to national sovereignty. He made the era's specific political issues fit his interpretation, like with his message "The Supreme Court Ruling on Prayer" (1962). Graham says that the court's ruling against school-sanctioned prayer "has touched at the very foundation of the American way of life," and he cites New York congressman John Rooney's reaction: "This ruling could put United States public schools on the same footing as the Soviet schools where any mention of the supreme being is not permitted."[41] Graham builds this message upon his idealized understanding of American history, saying that the Supreme Court's ruling could remove the foundational tenet of "one nation under God" from America's mental fabric (despite the phrase being legislated thanks to Graham's efforts less than a decade earlier).

The 1963 assassination of John F. Kennedy rocked the country, sparking national anxiety and unease that, when paired with ongoing Soviet nuclear militarization, brought the United States to an emotional tipping point. Graham moved swiftly to discuss the assassination ten days after the fact but used the moment to attack recent "anti-Christian" Supreme Court rulings. Graham offers a prescriptive apocalyptic solution to the pressing question of how an American president may be killed: "We have begun to realize that the collapse of our civilization, the disasters of our times, the moral disease with which we are afflicted, that all this is somehow the result of our departure from almighty God."[42] Thus, Kennedy died because America wandered from God. Graham then veers from explanation to worries over the Supreme Court and secular humanism. Allegations lacking evidence, and theological claims without scriptural support, pour from his lips, including the revelation that the government will force (unnamed) American schools to stop singing Christmas carols during the upcoming holiday season. America takes on a sort of social sickness that, in Graham's words, reflects an ever-growing spiritual malaise that shows how badly the nation depends on "In God We Trust."

World Aflame (1965) was Graham's first full-fledged apocalyptic book. He constructed it against the backdrop of American cultural and political unease surrounding the civil rights era, escalation of American involvement in the Vietnam War, and the end of the United States' involvement in the Korean War. *World Aflame* is a consummation of sorts for Graham's apocalyptic worldview up to that point. Nothing content-wise differs remarkably from preceding sermons and messages, but what makes this publication noteworthy is the absolute air with which Graham speaks. The introduction mentions threats like atomic weapons; misplaced blame for current struggles from economists, diplomats, sociologists, and other academics; and Graham's consistent solution to all worldly woes (individual and national repentance through Jesus Christ). However, Graham, like other evangelicals, presents his scriptural interpretations as normative and writes with confident certainty about his book's rationale and purpose:

> In this book my thesis is based on the Biblical philosophy
> of man and of history. The more I have traveled around the
> world the more convinced I have become that the Biblical
> revelation about man, his origin, his present predicament,

and his destiny is true. . . . Man is precisely what the Bible says he is. Human nature is behaving exactly as the Bible said it would. The course of human events is flowing just as Christ predicted it would.[43]

Graham clarifies that, to him, the book is *not* merely his understanding of the world's looming end; rather, he is simply the vessel through which the Bible's prophecies become known.

Graham weaves American exceptionalism throughout *World Aflame* and makes bold statements buttressing bold nationalistic sentiment:

America has probably been the most successful experiment in history. The American dream was a glorious attempt. It was built on a religious foundation. Its earliest concepts came from Holy Scripture. God honored and blessed America as few nations in history. However, in recent years the nation has been moving away from its religious heritage. Whether it knows it or not, it is in deep trouble both at home and abroad.[44]

One could argue that American colonization and military industrialization shaped the world and thus carry blame for the global political situation of the 1960s; that, however, is not what Graham means when he claims America faces global and local troubles. Graham instead blames American spiritual "schizophrenia," where "we have 'In God We Trust' on our coins but 'Me First' engraved on our hearts."[45]

World Aflame deviates from Graham's earlier sermons by citing more Scripture and offering insight into which apocalyptic scriptural preferences are operative for the evangelist. Up to this point, Graham had called for personal and national spiritual repentance but little else in terms of structural change that would alleviate the burdens of war, poverty, and injustice. He uses Daniel 2:34-35 to justify this position:

But when the Kingdom of God is established, it will not be established by social reforms, democratic principles, or scientific achievement alone. It will be established by the hand

of God in the midst of *the ruins* of our social and governmental institutions. This establishment is pictured in many
places in the Bible. One of the most graphic is the prophecy
of Daniel, who saw the culmination of God's Kingdom on
earth as an act of God and an event originating in heaven.[46]

Perhaps what is most surprising about Graham's thesis and explanation is just how unremarkable his work with Daniel and Revelation is when compared to other evangelical interpreters and
evangelists. Further, Graham's apocalyptic receptions, though
heralded by prominent American Christians and political leaders, are quite typical of Western evangelical Christian traditions
in content, form, function, and execution. Despite this com-
monplace nature, Graham's apocalyptic worldview would persist thanks to his political and social clout and, as the Vietnam
conflict escalated into total war, Graham molded interpretations
to keep them historically relevant. He reused and relabeled the
same scriptural passages and ideas from the 1940s and 1950s to
fit events and people of the late 1960s through the 1980s.

The Vietnam War and Its Aftermath: 1966–1983

Graham's rhetoric took another noticeable shift as his global popularity grew. In early apocalyptic sermons from the late 1940s and
the 1950s, he was vehemently anticommunist and proactively
pro-American. However, as he expanded his international footprint, his preaching location affected his content, as shown in the
1966 sermon given in West Berlin, "Christ Shall Return." Gone
are fanatical American trappings and any semblance of American
endurance ensured by Scripture, replaced by a calmer, more reas-
suring Graham who talks about Italy's catastrophic flooding with
promises of Christ's redemptive return. Graham even considers
Greek words used to describe Christ's return in the New Testament, perhaps to be more inviting to his international audience.

Despite his ease with international audiences, Graham's
speaking to American audiences prompted his return to familiar
"America first" apocalyptic language, especially as he built upon

the 1967 Israeli Six-Day War to justify his end-time prophetic proclamations. Unlike "Christ Shall Return" in 1966 and its warm invitation to participate in Jesus' global salvation, Graham put evangelical teeth in his 1967 message "Preparation for Armageddon." Here, Graham scales back nationalistic rhetoric (but maintains disdain for Soviet communism), beseeching America to return to God, and he focuses on individual conversion, saying that no existing panacea can alleviate the trials and tribulations besetting the world.[47]

The Vietnam War got messier as 1967 rolled on, and Graham's apocalyptic dread pressed forward:

> The war in Vietnam is going badly. The Castro Conference in Havana is openly planning revolution, not only in Latin America but in the United States as well. American gold reserves fell again in the month of July and racial violence continued to plague almost every part of the nation. Never in American history have we been told by our leaders that we never had it so good, when in fact, we've never had it so bad.[48]

Just like the 1940s and 1950s, Graham sees the late 1960s as *the* deciding era in U.S. history because "a free democratic society is now in the balance."[49] Nuance creeps into this sermon through additional evidence that Graham offers ample evidence for America's decline, including race protests in Detroit, Newark, and Milwaukee, which he calls the product of "extremists and subversive elements now at work in this country."[50] Graham describes the protestors as criminals, thugs, and roaming mobs, decrying their plight, and he sides with Supreme Court Justice Hugo Black's appeal to limit an individual's right to protest.

Against this historical background, Graham preached "Shadows of the Great Antichrist," a culmination of sorts for Graham's 1960s apocalyptic conflation of biblical texts. He reads Daniel 7 as predicting the antichrist, saying that the antichrist is the horn (at verses 11 and 20) that rules until the Ancient of Days' arrival in verse 22. Graham then equates Jesus' words in the Gospels, Paul's writings foretelling Jesus' return, and Jesus' arrival in

Revelation as fulfilling Daniel 7's prediction, which is yet again a standard evangelical apocalyptic tactic. Just as he did before, Graham claims that "the conflict of the ages" now unfolds and that 1967 is the end-times scenario Daniel describes.[51] The most puzzling addition Graham makes to this up-to-date apocalyptic take is what he calls "a spiritual invasion."[52] He claims minor antichrists work in secret to establish themselves and create free rein for the final antichrist, then pivots hard: "Satan's advance guard, emissaries from outer space, are now in the world. We are the victim of a spirit invasion."[53] Graham is quite literal here, arguing that the antichrist will be a physical person and that those so-called "emissaries from outer space" are physical beings infiltrating humanity to spread satanic influence through blasphemous, theological, and "wonder-working" antichrist-influenced authorities.[54] It seems that even Graham cannot resist influence from the late 1960s space race.

In his sermon "Can America Survive?" the 1968 presidential election prompts Graham to again claim that American democracy hangs in the balance. Unlike previous sermons, including those from the early 1960s, Graham gives the American political system greater credit and argues that one possible solution for America's ills, mainly the Vietnam War and ongoing civil rights work, is electing "men with the wisdom of Solomon and courage of David, prophets like Elijah, Jeremiah, and Amos."[55] He also discusses the New Hampshire presidential primaries in "Turning Point of a Nation" (1968) to consider physical and earthly needs like poverty, famine, and bodily violence, but only so that he can couch them under the umbrella of greater spiritual renewal. Thus, the older Graham got and the more political connections he made, the more credence he lent political systems. For example, Graham's sermon "America's Greatest Need" (1969) declares that America's "moral decadence" has "shocked the world," and he claims that, during his recent global travels, people were asking, "What's happening to America?"—meaning that America's condition puts the world on notice and warrants concern.[56] Graham wants his listeners to believe that the world is American-centric and America dependent. He claims that America needs "repentance" before citing sexual promiscuity and sinful living, and not the Vietnam War or ongoing civil rights struggles, as America's "open rebellion against God."[57]

Graham rolled into the 1970s with considerable momentum in globalizing his American-centric apocalyptic worldview. One maneuver he took, either accidentally or with intent, is a theological apocalyptic back-and-forth between individual salvation as the key to social stability and the fruitlessness of human structures in creating anything other than a world doomed for failure. In "The Coming Kingdom," he describes human failures at attempting economic and social utopias to argue that each human heart carries the metaphorical "cancer" of sin. He then equates the United Nations and defunct League of Nations with Genesis and the Tower of Babel and justifies this stance by saying that all earthly kingdoms "are under the influence of Satan."[58] Unlike previous sermons, Graham addresses racial issues directly, saying that "the greatest of all racial issues" is "whether we belong to the new race [of Christianity] or only to the old race of sinful humanity."[59]

"America, Is the Handwriting on the Wall?" (1973) is one of Graham's most popular sermons, and he preached variations of it throughout his career. The sermon is also one of his most direct in its use of Daniel and Revelation. Graham begins by reading Daniel, saying, "I suppose more than any other book of the Bible, this book predicts the future . . . unless it's the book of Revelation."[60] Graham urges his audience to approach Daniel and Revelation as one narrative to understand global affairs and to take their historical contents quite literally. He shares a story about a 1972 visit with the shah of Iran, and how he reminded the shah that "the first prime minister of ancient Persia was Daniel because Daniel was the first prime minister when the Medo-Persians came in and took over."[61] Potential inaccuracies from Graham's biblical historical claims aside, this sermon is perhaps the most definitive articulation of his 1970s apocalyptic worldview:

> You that are leaders of our world that do not give God the glory, and do not put your trust totally in him, and think that you can solve the problems yourself, you're going to come down! According to the scriptures, and the scriptures are very clear about it: whosoever shall exalt himself . . . shall be brought down, said Jesus.[62]

Graham uses threatening tones, which is an abrupt shift from his firm yet collected prescriptive language of the 1960s. Such a shift in Graham's vocal delivery is a return to form from the 1940s and 1950s, making "Handwriting" more of an apocalyptic diatribe and less of a sermon. True to this vacillating tactic of the 1970s, Graham uses American-focused language to warn world leaders, saying that America has fallen prey to self-imposed ease and luxury to become like Babylon in Daniel 5. Graham sees impending destruction, but, unlike his 1940s and 1950s apocalyptic messages, he couches these claims and says the physical world will not end; rather, it will be "the end of an age that is dominated by evil."[63]

Graham kept this global-yet-still-American focus with the book *Approaching Hoofbeats: The Four Horsemen of the Apocalypse* (1983) to offer a thorough reading of Revelation that focused on Revelation 6 and the titular four horsemen. He tells the reader that he writes *Hoofbeats* for the same reason John of Patmos wrote Revelation:

> With John, I have heard the distant sound of hoofbeats. I have the seen the evil riders on the horizons of our lives. I am still an evangelist whose one call is to proclaim new life in Christ, but there is serious trouble ahead for our world, for all of us who live in it, and in the four horsemen of the Apocalypse there is both a warning and wisdom for those troubled days ahead.[64]

Graham then dissects Revelation and claims that it is indeed a history book with two crucial messages regarding the apocalypse: "First, we learn that the judgement of the four horsemen is in part conditional. . . . Second, we learn that the judgment of the four horsemen is correctional."[65] The first point pushes against dispensational readings that argue the apocalypse date is preset and unchanging, as Graham presents an evangelical case for the timeline of God's final judgment being conditional: "God delays His judgments, possibly even for several generations, because many have listened to His message of warning and turned to Him in repentance and faith."[66] The next point, however, aligns with evangelical standards because judgements are not punishments: "They are meant to remind us forcefully of our need of God and the demand to follow His principles for living."[67] Seeing divine judgement as inevitable and negotiable is the essence of Graham's apocalyptic lens throughout the 1980s. This essence motivated his fiery sermons designed to compel change and American national repentance to delay God's wrath. His apocalyptic lens also illuminates Graham's Christology and eschatology, as he wanted listeners to avoid eternal damnation in the immediate present with personal salvation. This approach, it seems, would pacify God and allow more people an opportunity for repentance and belief.

Into the Current Era: 1984–2018

One would think that Graham would find a compelling ally in American apocalyptic thought with Reagan becoming president in 1980, and that Reagan's 1984 reelection would make the evangelist more zealous and impassioned. However, the opposite obtained, and Graham's rhetoric softened and his apocalyptic gusto became almost lethargic. Sermons from the mid-1980s until his death show that the once-emboldened pastor dropped vitriolic and absolutist language for a more approachable but still thoroughly American apocalyptic paradigm. How and why Graham changed is debatable and highly speculative, but one cannot deny that the fallout from Nixon and Watergate that rocked the nation also changed Graham.

Hypothetical questions appear frequently in Graham's sermons, so it is noteworthy when he asks his 1984 Bristol, England, audience, "Do you believe the world is coming to an end?" and then offers an immediate "A lot of people do" response.[68] He calmly states, "A lot of people believe it's maybe going to come to an end before the end of this century," and, instead of raising his voice or vocal cant, he stays placid.[69] He touches on the long history of people saying or proclaiming the world's coming end, even incorporating flood stories from the ancient Near East and Hebrew Bible. Early Graham would use such an opportunity to speak on the immediate and urgent need to become Christian and make America follow precise Christian pathways, but here he says that God withholds the coming end out of mercy for individuals who have yet to proclaim Jesus as their messiah.

Newfound language of opportunity, as opposed to obligation, has shifted Graham's apocalyptic rhetoric from direct and abrasive to roundabout and mild, though he retains some of his old flair when he says, "The only bright spot I can see in the future for the world is the coming again of Jesus Christ."[70] It now appears pointless to consider specifics, as Graham emphasizes Noah's patience alongside New Testament passages like Matthew 24:36-44 to lobby for visiting the imprisoned and the sick and "to do all kinds of things to help the people that are starving in Africa or Asia or wherever."[71] The "here and now" takes higher priority compared to sermons from decades before, as Graham realizes that the world may not end tomorrow. Thus, he deems it wise to encourage his flock to prepare to live longer than just a few weeks after his sermons.

Graham's interpretations of Daniel underline his mid-1980s apocalyptic softening, as his sermon "Daniel: A Religious Revolutionary" (1985) sheds apocalyptic trappings in favor of reading Daniel as an exemplar of righteous self-control and piety. Daniel becomes *the* "in-the-world but not-of-the-world" illustration that

Graham encourages his audience to mimic. Talk of social revolution only comes near the sermon's end, and Graham only speaks generally, telling his audience that the nation needs a "spiritual" revolution that young people can orchestrate through prayer and personal piety. Yet Graham's rhetorical force in "Dare to Be a Daniel" (1987) echoes his early impassioned zeal and nationalistic apocalyptic focus, when he storms out of the gate with news about Iraq considering the reconstruction of Babylon. Such news shakes Graham as he turns on the old flair and compares the rise and fall of ancient Babylon to America's current circumstances. Daniel 5 and Belshazzar's death are again his homiletical focus, and he makes rampant alcoholism the parallel between the fallen Babylonian ruler and American struggles. Graham ties excessive drinking to sexual excess ("There's over a million cases of incest every year in this country") but fails to support this specious claim with evidence beyond his own assessment.[72]

His last overtly apocalyptic book, *Storm Warning* (1992), is a thorough return to Graham's 1940s and 1950s form, as he opens by saying that Hurricane Andrew's landfall compels him to create something that will share "storm warnings of a different sort urging us to pay attention to the crises in our world." He also claims that humanity may be "staring blindly into the face of an oncoming storm of apocalyptic proportions."[73] Graham's apocalyptic paranoia in *Storm Warning* incorporates old 1950s and 1960s foes, including women's liberation, animal liberation, the sexual revolution, and other widespread cultural changes that "Greatest Generation" Americans scoff at or point to as disruptive and destructive. Politics remain a crucial metric, as he cites President George H. W. Bush's 1992 State of the Union address and the "undeniable awareness that something profound and unusual is happening in the world" because "the world has known changes of almost biblical proportions."[74]

Storm Warning hits Graham's standard apocalyptic beats and warns against complacency, saying that individual piety and redemption found in Jesus Christ is the world's only hope. The

Cold War's end, Germany's unification, and Saddam Hussein's defeat in Kuwait do not allay the ever-present warnings of famine, war, death, and encroaching chaos. However, unlike *Approaching Hoofbeats* (1983), *Storm Warning* is more of a general apocalyptic assessment than a book of Revelation commentary. Graham focuses on global political threats and cites unnamed secular "promoters of change" that "offer a grand vision of world unity" that brings the world "to the threshold of unparalleled peace and global oneness."[75] Like his disdain for the League of Nations, Graham opposes global unity because it does not come from Christian conviction. Such opposition may also stem from him being outside the world peace movement, meaning that if it happens without him, he does not want it to happen.

Graham preached and taught until his death, and, as age and sickness ravaged his body, his public appearances became calculated, intentional, and limited. A most telling statement about his retreat from the political limelight comes from a 2005 interview in which Graham forgoes his former political-apocalyptic zeal in favor of an "aw-shucks" approach to spreading Christianity: "If I get on these other subjects, it divides the audience on an issue that is not the issue I'm promoting. I'm just promoting the gospel."[76] Despite this apolitical cajoling, the 2011 revision of *Storm Warning* tells a different story as Graham eliminates global climate change as a threat that the original print from 1992 places alongside war, famine, and human ills. It also seems that Barack Obama's 2008 election alarms Graham, as the 2011 *Storm Warning* rerelease also talks about "clear evidence of a growing intolerance toward Christians and Christian values" in America.[77] Graham believes his idealized America is now gone (though he never really says it was ever "here"), as he claims (without evidence or formal support), "It is no longer as accepted to profess Christ as it once was in America."[78] This revision indeed contains many changes, some of them radical, as Graham uses recent natural disasters as contemporary signs of God's judgement and mercy designed to warn people about the future. Any hope Graham holds for state apparatuses becoming instruments of God's work seems lost as he bemoans how the America of the Marshall Plan, Dwight Eisenhower, and righteous economic prosperity is now an America of abortion, AIDS, and hedonism.

Graham the Consistent Apocalypticist

This chapter attempted to cover over sixty years of Graham's sermons to convey one point: American-centric apocalypticism based on interpretations of Daniel and Revelation was a major piece of Graham's rhetorical toolkit. Further, such an approach was a foundational cog in how, what, and why he preached. Building on this apocalyptic worldview, it is also clear that Graham viewed America as an apocalyptic cornerstone upon which the world's fate hinged. It is worth noting that Graham consistently heralded America's impending doom and claimed to believe that whatever moment he preached in was *the* moment upon which America's survival, and the world's well-being, pivoted. Yet despite his gloom-and-doom orientation, the country did not fall apart, nor did democracy disintegrate. Economic forces ebbed and flowed, presidents won and lost elections, people fought wars, and the world kept spinning. America maintained a position of political, military, and cultural prominence, but Graham continued espousing foreboding American-focused apocalyptic rhetoric. America's general stability and prosperity makes one wonder why Graham kept returning to apocalyptic theological or hermeneutical motivations. However, as audiences continued to fill auditoriums and buy his books, the financial, social, and political motives remained scandalously clear.

FOUR

PREACHER, PASTOR, AND PRESIDENT

Studying *how* something happens is the first step toward understanding *why* something happens. Therefore, before questioning why American presidents use "under God" for political gains, we must first understand how evangelicals came to place considerable political and social weight upon it. Further, we also need to investigate how Graham's apocalyptic nationalism became binding law through President Eisenhower's legislation of the now-infamous phrase. These two moves not only show the "how"; they also begin peeling back the many layers and players behind the morphing of "under God" into an unquestionable—and highly apocalyptic—American staple.

One Nation under Whose God?

Evangelical Christians imposed their fingerprints on "under God" long before the infamous 1954 legislation. For example, the first annual National Prayer Breakfast in 1953 gets much attention, given that it was the first time a large group of political figures (over five hundred)—including senators, representatives, and Supreme Court justices—gathered to answer Eisenhower's push to move America "Back to God."[1] One can also consider

Eisenhower's Christian baptism at the National Presbyterian Church and the impassioned Christian zeal the president brought to his presidency, becoming the first and still only president to be baptized in office. Yet what frequently goes unquestioned is the overtly evangelical Christian associations with all references to God during the nation's 1950s religious swell. When taken charitably, "one nation under God" may be read as pluralistic. One could argue that the God of which Americans speak is the same God that Muslims, Jews, and Christians worship, saying that "God" is common vernacular for one's chosen deity.

Such naïve pluralism, however, was quite far from the truth, as the God that Eisenhower compelled Americans to heed is remarkably Christian and profoundly evangelical. Eisenhower's remarks from December 1952, before taking office in January 1953, speak as much to this clear Christian orientation:

> And this is how they [the Founding Fathers in 1776] explained those: "we hold that all men are endowed by their Creator . . ." not by the accident of their birth, not by the color of their skins or by anything else, but "all men are endowed by their Creator." In other words, our form of government has no sense unless it is founded in a deeply felt religious faith, and I don't care what it is. With us of course it is the Judeo-Christian concept, but it must be a religion with all men are created equal.[2]

Thus, it is no surprise that at the 1953 event later known as the National Prayer Breakfast, Eisenhower returns to what he sees as the pressing need for national theological proclamation. He chooses his words tactfully, saying, "Today I think that prayer is just simply a necessity, because by prayer I believe we mean an effort to get in touch with the Infinite." One could argue that Eisenhower's use of "the Infinite" is ecumenical, but his audience betrays any sense of religious pluralism because he speaks to leaders from the International Christian Leadership group. Further, Eisenhower gave an address in July 1953 to the National Conference on Christians and Jews, a move imbued with evangelical zeal given that a key evangelical foundation was creating (and still maintains) close connections between the United States and the nation of Israel.[3] Thus, when Eisenhower speaks of a "God" or "religion," he speaks about the Christian deity and messianic claims that Christians make. This means that his push for "under God" focuses on building a national sentiment based on Christian belief in an all-knowing, all-powerful deity.

One need only consider America's immediate religious history to see evangelical indentions all over this "God." For example, to read Graham's 1940s and 1950s sermons alongside speeches from leaders like Eisenhower would prompt one to believe that America was an atheist wasteland following the Allied victory in WWII, devoid of any religious piety and spiritual growth. However, rudimentary data shows that not only were Graham and Eisenhower "preaching to the choir" with their religious rhetoric, but also American Christian church attendance skyrocketed in the late 1940s and early 1950s.[4] Further, one could also argue that Graham and Eisenhower carried no responsibility for the evangelical surge of the 1940s and 1950s; yet evidence can show that these two men rode that wave for political and cultural expediency.

Numbers show that pressure from Graham, Eisenhower, and other like-minded Christians backfired as church attendance peaked in the early 1960s but suffered a precipitous decline as the decade unfolded.[5] It seems using "under God" as an evangelical political totem and lightning rod payed only immediate dividends, as American church attendance lowered with each passing year, despite continued insistence from evangelical leaders that "under God" still bound the God-fearing nation together. Evangelical voices like Graham's wielded the phrase to oppose Soviet atheism and other "idolatrous" faiths from around the world. Graham continuously berated non-Christian nations like Saudi Arabia, Iran, and Iraq for their shortcomings, and he blamed their faults on misguided religious practices. With "under God," Graham and Eisenhower were not talking about some general, amorphous God meant to appease social anxieties and soothe personal challenges. Instead, they were talking about the Christian God, and instituted these two words into the national discourse with hope and trepidation. They hoped that the nation would follow their lead and "return" to God, but they hesitated to restrain their religious zeal out of fear for the very God they sought to praise. Thus, it seems an apt subtitle to "under God" would be "America: One Nation Under God . . . or Else."

Eisenhower's Religion

Many histories of Eisenhower's life and presidency exist, but each is highly selective in what it highlights and ignores. Like almost all histories of the United States, such reconstructions neglect dissonant historical realities to appear neutral. For example, students in American grade-school classrooms read about the nation's great World War II triumph over Nazi Germany and looked with scorn and horror upon Nazi beliefs like genetic superiority, eugenic sciences, and selective reproduction. However, the same students entered college classrooms and experienced shock upon learning that these same Nazis got their genetic science from American scientists who championed discriminatory human breeding and sterilization of persons deemed socially "unfit."

Such selective historical reconstructions drive this project because contemporary individual and communal histories forgo controversy in favor of more palatable recollections. The path of Graham's receptions from sermons to legislation involved people beyond Graham, including Eisenhower's family and the work of George Docherty, a little-known Presbyterian pastor. An examination of Dwight Eisenhower's religious life, his family, and their shared apocalyptic worldviews illuminates what made him susceptible to and comfortable with Graham's apocalyptic language. It also shows how Eisenhower connected with Docherty, a talented but previously unremarkable Scottish Presbyterian minister with ties to Graham, creating a triad between preacher, pastor, and president that still shapes American political and religious movements.

Eisenhower never denied being a religious man. Early correspondence to his son John shows that Eisenhower connected personal faith to military duty for country, combining the two as one guiding belief: "Never forget that in the soldier's life the first tenet of his religion must always be the immediate and proper performance of duty. Everything else is second to that."[6] Eisenhower also openly described America's WWII efforts in Tunisia as "a crusade in the traditional sense" because "only by the utter destruction of the Axis was a decent world possible."[7] As president, Eisenhower frequently rejected invitations to Sunday sporting events to avoid violating the Sabbath, repeatedly justifying this choice by saying it appeased "so many people in this country" who hold Sundays sacred.[8] Despite such clear spiritual language, Eisenhower withheld details about his religious past, and broader media coverage around Eisenhower's religion downplayed his family's religious history for a blander and nondescript "Christian" label.

The historical reality of Eisenhower's upbringing, however, is far from bland. Eisenhower's parents were devout and pious Christians that became members of the Watchtower Society, also known as Jehovah's Witnesses. Dwight's mother, Ida, joined the Witnesses in 1895 and soon after became a Witness minister.[9] This is remarkable given the rigor necessary to become a Watchtower Society minister, meaning that Ida's choice was no fleeting idea or passing thought; she made the movement her entire life. Ida recruited her husband, David, and, after that, the family hosted weekly Watchtower meetings and scriptural study in their home. Their sons, including Dwight, participated in the apocalyptic-focused Bible studies built upon the apocalyptic roots of the Jehovah's Witness movement.[10] Such involvement shows the widespread and genuine nature of Eisenhower's religious upbringing, as it defined his adolescent homelife.

Dwight's decision to attend the U.S. Military Academy at West Point divided his family, as Witness doctrine strictly forbids military service. Ida took Dwight's military decision hard, given her zeal for the movement, but she never excommunicated her son from the family, even as their relationship remained contentious, especially when Dwight's military success yielded global fame and recognition. Popularity also brought national scrutiny onto Dwight's personal and religious life, but the ever-careful Dwight played his cards well to paint the proper picture for his public persona. For example, a 1946 *Time* article downplayed Ida's Watchtower connections and presented the Eisenhower family as simply devout Christians rooted in the River Brethren Christian community. Active Witnesses responded to the article with direct contempt and objection, saying that Ida "was never a River Brethren. She was one of Jehovah's Witnesses," and that *Time*'s misrepresentation "was merely continuing [*Time*'s] consistent policy of slander in all that pertains to Jehovah's Witnesses."[11] The response continued, contending that, despite Ida's failing health later in life, "she remained a staunch believer" and that claiming anything else misrepresents Ida's true beliefs.[12]

Dwight downplayed his family's religious connections because apocalyptic language permeates Witness literature and defines their doctrine. Witnesses read Daniel and Revelation as undisguised end-time prophecies designed to help modern Witnesses prepare for creation's looming end. Witnesses frequently forgo higher education to spread the group's message and share their faith so that nonbelievers can avoid damnation through eternity in an earthly paradise free of disease, war, and death. One cannot help but hear echoes of Watchtower belief and doctrine when considering Eisenhower's use of Scripture and language about hope, dreams, and prosperity, as the words now ring with certain apocalyptic tenor. Reconsidering his reference to a "crusade" in his wartime letters and when he wrote, "My brothers and I devoutly believe in the extraordinary virtues of our parents," Eisenhower now speaks against the backdrop of Daniel, Revelation, and apocalyptic Watchtower teachings.[13]

Graham and Christian evangelists used Watchtower-like rhetoric to gain mainstream popularity, but Graham opposed

Witnesses as a Christian sect. He placed them alongside what he called deviant religious cults like the Church of Jesus Christ of Latter-day Saints, Unitarians, the Unification Church, Scientologists, and Spiritists.[14] Despite Graham's aversion to Jehovah's Witnesses, something in Eisenhower's background let him connect with Graham—as the metaphorical wall that President Harry S. Truman built to insulate himself from Graham's machinations disappeared, leaving space for an uncommon spiritual-political relationship between Eisenhower and Graham. That thing enabling this bond between president and preacher was without question Eisenhower's apocalyptic-oriented Jehovah's Witness upbringing, so when the pair met, Eisenhower was already an apocalyptic canvas on which Graham could paint.

President to Preacher: Eisenhower's Relationship with Graham

The journeys of Graham and Eisenhower to each other continued with the election of President Truman and America's subsequent response to nuclear anxieties. America's two atomic weapons that end World War II caused literal and figurative fallout, as the tactic settled the war on the Pacific front and made the United States the preeminent global military power. However, American atomic primacy changed at 11:08 a.m. on September 23, 1949, when Truman's White House released a statement confirming a successful Soviet atomic test. This press release shows that the relationship between America and the Soviet Union was now profoundly different, as the scales once favoring America now balanced with two global powers facing off for nuclear supremacy.

American panic ensued, which Graham tied to the successful Soviet nuclear test. He wove said nuclear panic into his sermons immediately, as, only two days after the news broke, Graham preached:

> Do you know the area that is marked out for the enemy's first atomic bomb? New York! Secondly, Chicago! City of

> Los Angeles! God is giving us a desperate choice, a choice of either revival or judgment. There is no alternative! . . . The world is divided: into one side we see Communism . . . [which] has declared against Christ, against the Bible, and against all religion! Unless the Western world has an old-fashioned revival, we cannot last![15]

Calling for and claiming that an American religious revival is *the* global political and nuclear solution gave Graham considerable public traction in his rise to stardom. Graham's remarkable cultural ascent yielded tangible political results, as his rallies, which he called "Crusades," occurred throughout the country, with stops on the East and West Coasts, throughout the Midwest, the Southern states, and the Northeast. Graham's words resounded across the nation like those of circuit preachers of old, as people came in droves to hear him. Over 350,000 people attended Graham's Los Angeles rally in 1949, with religious fervor stretching the original three-week gathering into an eight-week extravaganza.[16] Graham's radio presence also boasted considerable reach, as the *Hour of Decision* began broadcasting in 1950 on over 150 stations nationwide. Graham could now connect with millions of people, allowing his voice and sermons to ring from coast to coast.

Such public connections made Graham an opportunity for politicians to spread their message alongside his. Representative John McCormack of Massachusetts and Representative Joseph Bryson of South Carolina jumped on board with Graham and became close allies to the young evangelist. Graham's impact on McCormack and Bryson was so significant that the two representatives urged President Truman to meet with the then-thirty-one-year-old preacher. Graham himself also pushed hard to curry favor with Truman, frequently writing letters warning that Russian communism is "the greatest enemy we have ever known" and suggesting the solution lay in a great national Christian revival.[17] One cannot deny Graham's political shrewdness in seeking the president's public acknowledgment, as he also called local pastors to press Truman toward embracing Graham and his anti-Soviet, pro-America Christian gospel. Despite considerable tenacity, these efforts failed, and Truman ignored Graham's contact. Truman's response only spurred Graham to double down on his American exceptionalist readings of Daniel and Revelation, saying that no enemy could destroy the American people if they turned to God and that "our way of life can be saved" through religious revival.[18] Graham's sermons and radio broadcasts during his struggle with Truman reflect an "if only" quality, as Graham told his audiences that the keys to American success and stability were available if their leaders would only comply with God's will.

Graham repeatedly claimed that unnamed politicians and leaders were the only things blocking utopian prosperity. Viewed alongside Truman's apprehensions toward him, these words clearly point to Truman. Yet simply studying Truman's religiosity from speeches and writings shows that the thirty-third president was no atheist or antireligion shill. Truman mentions "God" three times in his 1949 inaugural address: First, he claims that freedom is a human right since "all men are created equal because they are created in the image of God." Second, he says that the fight between democracy and communism extends beyond American soil: "People everywhere are coming to realize that what is involved is material well-being, human dignity, and the right to believe in and worship God." Third, he concludes the speech by urging his audience to rely on God in the struggle for peace: "With God's help, the future of mankind will be assured in a world of justice, harmony, and peace."[19] Despite explicit Christian-centric theological sentiment, Graham felt that Truman failed in the spiritual battle that threatened the world as he doggedly pursued the president to be more public and more particular in his faith. For Graham, it was not enough to talk about God, because the people and nations that prosper in Daniel and Revelation are those that shout God's name from the highest places as their nations live to serve under God.

President Truman finally agreed to meet Graham in 1950 with one major condition: no notes or pictures of the conversation would be released to the public. For Truman, the meeting was a public pleasantry at best and a time-wasting annoyance at worst. The president wanted the zealous evangelist to have his say and stop annoying the leader of the free world. Graham, however, saw the meeting as a proof of concept: pressure put upon Truman proved the importance of Graham's mission and message and suggested that with similar dogged persistence America could endure and thrive. After their conversation, Graham spited Truman's request about records and pictures by posing for a picture in a kneeled, prayerful position on the White House lawn with three men (G. F. Beavan, Cliff Burrows, and Grady Wilson) that Graham brought to the meeting. The picture went viral, prompting Truman's ire and frustration as Graham did the very thing the Truman sought to avoid. Graham's tactic worked. He now had access to national and global leaders, meaning that his apocalyptic receptions of biblical texts, interpretations, and ideas could reach national and international audiences. Graham's pursuit of Truman shows that the evangelist would not go away quietly, and the president set a standard of acquiescence as Graham now held a permanent seat at the political table.

Graham amplified his American nationalist rhetoric in 1951 to garner public favor after Truman's contentious dismissal of General Douglas MacArthur. According to Truman, the general "didn't respect the authority of the President," and, despite significant national sentiment opposing MacArthur, Graham championed that segment of the American public that decried the dismissal.[20] Graham began speaking openly against American leadership and claimed that the current trajectory paved the road for American destruction at the hands of antireligious Soviet communists. Truman simply could not win with Graham. Anytime Truman gave a little, Graham kept demanding more. It would be a relationship on Graham's terms, or there would be no relationship at all.

Unlike with Truman, Graham grew close to then-general Eisenhower during Eisenhower's presidential run. Graham still preached theological nationalism, rejected communism, and made American capitalism a bastion of cosmic stability during Eisenhower's rise to the presidency. He also imbued Eisenhower with messianic power to claim that spiritual warfare between "good" American capitalism and "bad" Soviet socialism awaited the future president: "The people are hungry for a moral crusade, and they need a Moses or Daniel to lead them in this hour."[21] Calling for Eisenhower to be a Moses or Daniel inverted a classic trope that other Christian interpreters have employed: rather than assigning specific adversarial figures to Daniel and Revelation's fantastical images, Graham identified Eisenhower with Daniel himself. To Graham, Eisenhower was the American messiah that would ward off Soviet communism and, in turn, the antichrist.

Eisenhower said what Graham wanted a leader to say; he did what Graham wanted an American leader to do; and, in Graham's eyes, he led how God would have a man like Moses or Daniel lead. Graham changed his apocalyptic receptions from gloom and doom to optimism and positivity, reading Eisenhower's possible presidency as a beacon of hope and prayerful fulfillment. This was not an accident, as Eisenhower revealed years later in a conversation with oil baron Sid Richardson that Graham was instrumental in getting him to run for president. Eisenhower claimed that Graham's letter imploring him to clean out Washington or face "a period of chaos that could bring about our downfall" tipped Eisenhower's decision.[22] Eisenhower's religious background was now his own, as Witnesses staunchly oppose formal relationships with government forces, but Graham's influence on Eisenhower's decision to run shows the power Graham had over him.

Critics initially assailed Eisenhower's Witness history, saying that he was an "anti-Christian cultist" and "foe of patriotism."[23] Yet what some saw as adversarial Graham used as an opportunity, leading to Eisenhower becoming Graham's gold standard for Christian leadership. Their relationship spanned Eisenhower's presidency as the pair spoke often about major issues, including and especially American civil rights.[24] For example, Eisenhower sought Graham's advice about the young up-and-coming Baptist preacher Martin Luther King Jr., and used Graham as a spiritual mind through which Eisenhower could navigate King's movement. It is very telling that Eisenhower confided in Graham about King instead of reaching out to King himself, making Graham's impact undeniable as his path from spiritual guide to political advisor was now complete.

Graham reciprocated Eisenhower's trust by lionizing the president to godlike status. For example, in the 1953 sermon "Mr. President," he compares Eisenhower's speeches to the Sermon on the Mount, saying that a "spiritual deluge" threatens the planet and that only warfare through spreading a pro-American capitalist Christian gospel will eliminate communist threats.[25] Graham elevates spiritual revival above military triumph while reminding his audience about Eisenhower's theological priorities, telling the audience that Eisenhower had a Bible open during his inauguration to the "Heal their land" passage in 2 Chronicles. Graham then emphasizes that the battle between Soviet communism and American capitalist is cosmic, meaning that the world's fate lies in the spiritual revival that Eisenhower could bring.

Graham counts his relationship with Eisenhower as a victory and intimates as much in *Storm Warning*:

> During the 1950s, it was my privilege to be a friend of Dwight D. Eisenhower both before and after he served as president of the United States. I hope I had some influence on him, and certainly he had a strong impact on my thinking.[26]

Graham then cites Eisenhower's "The Chance for Peace" (1953), also known as the "Cross of Iron" speech, as evidence for Graham's influence on Eisenhower's thought and rhetoric. Graham demonstrates his bond with Eisenhower, saying words from that very speech that compelled Graham and his colleagues to visit "developing countries."[27] But what is most important to this book is that the impact that Graham's relationship had on Eisenhower came on full display on Flag Day, June 14, 1954, when Eisenhower legislated the official inclusion of "under God" in the Pledge of Allegiance. The decision to change the pledge to include Christian theological language came from a joint resolution between the president and Congress to combat what Graham, Eisenhower, Eisenhower's peers, and American voters understood as Russia's anti-American, atheist, and communist ideologies. Eisenhower signed and committed to "under God" without irony or insincerity, saying:

> In this way we are reaffirming the transcendence of religious faith in America's heritage and future; in this way we shall constantly strengthen those spiritual weapons which forever will be our country's most powerful resource, in peace or war.[28]

The president continued:

> From this day forward the millions of our school children will proclaim daily in every city and town, every village and rural school house, the dedication of our nation and our people to the Almighty.[29]

Eisenhower sounds much like Graham here: American religious revival is now key to defeating communism, making the spiritual battle just as important as any literal battle. Thus, Graham's preaching and teaching found their way into the words and sentiments of an American president. Eisenhower used this language to justify legislating a phrase dedicated to the Christian God, affecting the hearts and minds of present and future Americans.

Graham's apocalyptic influenced and shaped Eisenhower's perspective about the need for an American spiritual revival and, in so doing, changed the Pledge of Allegiance itself. But the relationship between Eisenhower and Graham tells only part of the story about what unfolded on that 1954 Flag Day. It is perhaps Graham's greatest stroke of genius, coincidence, or possibly some combination of both that his apocalyptic influence came at the president from two fronts: first, from Graham himself, and second, from the Presbyterian pastor George Docherty.

President to Pastor: Eisenhower's Relationship with Rev. George Docherty

On February 7, 1954, Rev. Dr. George Docherty preached a sermon at New York Avenue Presbyterian Church in Washington, D.C., that changed the world. In the sermon, he spoke of America's special place among nations and of its duty to them, and he maintained that the only way to ensure American prosperity—and, in turn, global stability—would be to bring the nation back to God. Docherty's words that day still shape American religious, political, and social landscapes because, after that sermon, President Eisenhower felt personally compelled to incorporate "under God" into the Pledge of Allegiance. But the journey behind Docherty's sermon that day and its American exceptionalist attitude carries the influence of one man: Billy Graham. Before Graham, Docherty was a Scottish-born Presbyterian pastor simply doing his job serving churches as a pastor. After Graham, Docherty's preaching was evangelistic, as he laced it with American devotion filled with patriotic passion. An examination of their relationship shows how Graham's apocalyptic nationalism pulled Docherty into an evangelical frenzy over Graham's apocalyptic zeal. It is this very zeal and not a general theological inclination that spurred Docherty to preach that sermon on that February day with Eisenhower in attendance.

Originally from Glasgow, Scotland, Docherty came to the United States to serve the New York Avenue Presbyterian Church. The church's previous claim to fame was a tradition known as "Lincoln Day," in which sitting presidents trekked to the modest building and attended services on the Sunday closest to President Abraham Lincoln's birthday. This meant that for at least one Sunday per calendar year, the person standing behind that pulpit held direct access to one of the world's most powerful people, and when Eisenhower visited on February 7, 1954, the minister from Scotland took advantage and preached a thundering sermon. Docherty called the nation and its leaders to embrace an American-centric divine birthright—or else. He filled his message with anti-Soviet rhetoric, framing the battle between the economic ideologies as spiritual and theological in its motivation and culmination. Existence itself hung in the balance.

This sermon worked as Graham's ideas poured from Docherty's mouth, giving new life to the evangelist's nationalistic footprint. On the very next day, February 8, 1954, Michigan representative Charles Oakman introduced a bill to formally (and legislatively) put "under God" into the Pledge of Allegiance. Oakman mentioned Docherty and this sermon directly: "Mr. Speaker, I think Mr. Docherty hit the nail squarely on the head. One of the most fundamental differences between us and the Communists is our belief in God."[30] Similarly, on March 8, 1954, Senator Homer Ferguson buttressed his call for adding "under God" to the pledge and cited Docherty's "Lincoln Day" sermon.[31] But it is in considering Docherty's inspiration that Graham comes roaring into the fold, pulling the discussion away from Docherty's ideology and into Graham's machinations. Many historical retellings confirm that Docherty's sermon indeed steered Eisenhower, but that is only half the story. Docherty preached that day to fulfill a calling for national repentance instilled by Graham himself in 1952, thereby completing a journey that began with theological skepticism but ended in Christian nationalism.

Docherty knew and had heard of Graham's exploits, and it was because of this national brand that the Presbyterian minister initially regarded Graham as shallow and flashy. And yet, only one event changed that relationship into one of deep respect and admiration. It started with an invitation to the 1952 "Billy Graham Washington Campaign" that called the Presbyterian minister to join the Southern evangelical leader at a rally in Washington, D.C. Graham personally requested that Docherty sit next to him on the platform. In his sermon, "Prepare to Meet Thy God," Graham declared that "men will be governed by God or by tyrants."[32] Graham continued to preach on American exceptionalist ideas throughout the rally and spoke directly to political leaders: "I beg of you American leaders who are here today, the millions that are listening to my voice by radio, that you humble yourselves, confess your sins, and turn to God while there is time."[33] Though Graham preached to a large crowd in person and on the radio during the rally, Docherty recalled feeling that God was using Graham to speak to him and him alone:

> Then it happened. To this day I cannot articulate the nature of the emotion that was slowly, imperceptibly, but surely beginning to take me over. The marvelous voice and its ringing sincerity were beginning to seep into the into the inner ear of my soul. The fantastic exegesis no longer seemed important. Behind the words I could hear another Voice, in an accent I shall never know this side of Calvary, saying to me . . . in a still small voice, "And how stands it with you, my son?" In Billy's presence I was seeing my own ministry and preaching, and what I was looking at was not very pleasant.[34]

What happened that day between Docherty and Graham was nothing short of a conversion experience that changed Docherty's preaching, teaching, and theology in profound ways. Docherty was a learned and intelligent man, well versed in Scripture and doctrine, but he was no match for Graham's natural charisma and charm as the evangelist wove a tapestry of America as the sole protector of celestial stability.

No longer a skeptic to Graham's call for national repentance, Docherty sang Graham's praises, modeled how he preached after Graham's style and content, and became sharply American-centric in his theology. He frequently rushed to Graham's public defense against criticism from Christian pastors, like Dr. Powell Davis after Davis published a letter in the *Washington Post* critical of Graham and mass evangelism. Docherty responded and gave Graham prophetic credit by claiming that Graham only called out preexisting guilt and sin and that the nation would be wise to heed Graham's words. Docherty's letter reached Graham, prompting the evangelist to again reach out to Docherty. The two were soon close confidants, as what began with an invitation to a rally was now a relationship that granted Graham greater influence on Eisenhower's religious spirit. The next step for the journey of Graham's American apocalypticism was complete: the man who preached a sermon on the importance of "one nation under God" to President Eisenhower became that man after hearing Graham's American-apocalyptic message. Without Graham's influence, Docherty's sermon simply would not have happened. If not for that sermon, the life of "under God" would have played out quite differently.

Docherty also connected Graham to President Abraham Lincoln, as he described the Gettysburg Address and Lincoln's charge for America to be a nation "under God" as evidence to compel others about America's need for religious reform: "Without the words *under God*, the Pledge of Allegiance seemed to me quite secular; it could have been repeated by any little Muscovite who cared to replace the phrase 'the United States of America' with 'the Union of Soviet Socialist Republics.'"[35] Docherty completed this circle between his sermon in February 7, 1954, the Gettysburg Address, and his admiration for Graham when he drew comparison between his idealized reconstruction of the sixteenth president and Graham, describing Graham at the fateful 1952 rally as a "reclining statuesque . . . Lincoln figure" holding "a large black soft-leather-bound King James Bible."[36] Graham and the Christian America that Graham fantasized about infatuated Docherty. Just as Docherty saw Lincoln change and protect a volatile nation, so did the Scottish minister hear Graham as a beacon of hope and bastion of spiritual stability amid global tumult. These things inspired the message that Docherty preached on Lincoln Day, 1954, as the interpretations of Daniel and Revelation that Docherty espoused prompted an American president to legislate a nationwide expression of allegiance. Such devotion paired with the connection between Graham and Lincoln—a presidential figure that many Americans consider to be one of the greatest presidents, if not the greatest president, in the young nation's history—shows that Graham was Docherty's own personal Abraham Lincoln.

This potent combination of patriotic ideals with apocalyptic sentiment took Graham's 1952 sermon from that stage in Washington, D.C., and imprinted it on President Eisenhower through Docherty's sermon, paving the way for "under God" to carry Graham's apocalyptic worldview across the fabric of American culture. Graham was indeed a popular figure and *the* rising star in the global evangelical landscape, but one must ask why Docherty so quickly abandoned his critical lens toward mass evangelistic crusades. What magic did Graham employ that so effectively swept Docherty into the evangelist's apocalyptic fold? The answer is quite simple. Graham's American-centric Christian rhetoric showed Docherty the path to the one thing he did not have, the one thing that he came to want very desperately: Graham made Docherty feel like an American.

And yet, like America experiencing declining zeal (following the failures in Vietnam, the scandals of Watergate, and the costs of the Cold War), so Docherty eventually changed his theological and political orientations. Unlike Graham, Docherty actively participated in the civil rights movement, marched on Selma with Dr. Martin Luther King Jr., and joined Dr. King in protesting America's military involvement in Vietnam. Docherty even walked back his initial American-exceptionalist ardor inspired by Graham, saying in 1984:

> I still consider my reasoning to be valid but the times should have overruled my philosophical arguments as irrelevant in light of the greater issues at hand. A false patriotism was being aroused by the bogus threat of Communist encroachment; McCarthyism darkened the airwaves; superpatriots were prone to ask not whether they were on God's side, but whether God was on theirs.[37]

In the face of Docherty's later apprehensions, the work was complete, and Graham's efforts paid off. Graham used Docherty's position to further Graham's apocalyptic political goals, which explains why Docherty's later life shows someone more than willing to combat social issues. He knew that Graham's passion and charisma had roped him into the tides of American exceptionalism. Because of Docherty, Graham's impact was permanent, and "one nation under God" became a de facto slogan for the United States of America. Despite Docherty's change of heart, Graham's influence had just begun.

Three Leaders, Three Relationships, One Pledge

Things were never the same after the events that allowed Graham's voice to come through Docherty's lips. Eisenhower and Graham became close allies, Docherty and Graham were friends, and Docherty felt a sense of divine accomplishment for his efforts. These three relationships created one pledge that would stand the test of time and that blurred lines between religious freedom and sectarian compulsion. Further, including "under God" in an official capacity prompted minimal pushback from the American people. The American Civil Liberties Union avoided the issue and waited on church leaders to defend church-state separation, though one official declared, "I doubt whether any such leaders would make this statement."[38] Similarly, progressive Christian magazine *Christian Century* noted the national apathy to the "under God" legislation and published an article, "Constitutional Amendments and Religious Liberty," in which its author argued that it "is the sort of proposal against which no member of Congress would think of voting, any more than against a resolution approving of motherhood."[39] Such distressingly light opposition only illuminated America's Christian bias alongside the spotty implementation of the Constitution's First Amendment protections for religious freedom and expression. Quite simply, legislating "under God" got a free pass because it came from and spoke for the nation's Christian majority.

One can hear contemporary church and state issues echoing throughout this shockingly bipartisan approval that theologized an expression of nationalistic and political allegiance. It reflects the possible life of any text or idea, as some interpretations become so ingrained in our collective subconsciousness that we cannot separate interpretation from the text itself. Make no mistake, the Pledge of Allegiance is an interpretation, and that interpretation is overtly apocalyptic. But one cannot discount the subtle brilliance in Graham's interpretive approach, as his apocalyptic language paired with homegrown Southern cultural resonance to appear less threatening. Graham told audiences day after day, night after night, that their behaviors condemned the entire world to eternal damnation, while arenas continued to fill and books kept flying off shelves. This shows just how accessible Graham's apocalypticism had become, and that same accessibility allowed a Presbyterian minister from Scotland to see visions of Abraham Lincoln in Graham's pulpit. It also made Docherty not think twice about reiterating the same message from his pulpit with the president as his audience. Graham now wielded a decisive resource with Eisenhower's legislation—his evangelical apocalyptic dread was a warm embrace that the nation could not resist.

One cannot overstate the importance of what unfolded in 1954 between Graham, Docherty, and Eisenhower. Because of Eisenhower's power and position, an idea that Graham fierily preached from pulpits in meeting halls and churches now came from the mouths of children in classrooms and from adults in public gathering places, really, any situation in which people recited the pledge. Moreover, Eisenhower further solidified the place of Graham's interpretation and ideology into the annals of American history when he signed P.L. 84-140 into law on July 30, 1956, which mandated "In God We Trust" as the nation's official motto and that the phrase be printed on all paper money. With this, Graham's xenophobic reading of Daniel and Revelation lives on as Americans recite the pledge and spend their money, with most citizens being completely unaware of the phrase's origin. On the surface, they recite a simple set of poetic lines dedicated to instilling Americans with a spirit of unity and comradery.

Deeper still, however, sits Graham's passion to defend America and his understanding of what "America" represents. The pledge allowed his reception to live on and become synonymous with America itself, as individual citizens saw the pledge as a symbol that warded off evils like communism, feminism, and all things Graham deemed un-American.

Apocalyptic anxieties continued to haunt Graham before the 1960 presidential election. Graham returned to nationalistic fire and vitriol after Eisenhower shared that Russia shot down an American U-2 spy plane in May 1960: "We may be living at the end of history."[40] On top of the spy plane incident, Graham also vehemently opposed then-senator John F. Kennedy during the 1960 presidential election, believing that a Catholic was unfit for presidential power and saying that election was "the most crucial our nation has ever confronted."[41] Graham harbored obvious anti-Catholic sentiment and made an overt tie to Revelation when he reiterated his position against Kennedy and for then-candidate Richard Nixon, saying that the nation was "wrestling with the forces of the anti-Christ" and that the voting public should "not decide on the basis of which candidate is more handsome or charming."[42] This remark about Kennedy's appearance carried considerable evangelical apocalyptic flavor, as countless sermons, Bible studies, and books unpack the unknown "appeal" the antichrist will have and how this draw will make people overlook glaring inconsistencies in that figure's life and work. For Graham, Kennedy's handsome features only made him more of a threat. And yes, despite harboring such overt animosity toward Kennedy's candidacy, Graham's anxieties about Kennedy all but vanished when the popular young president took office. Such change does not mark a shift in the relationship between Graham and Kennedy; instead, it confirms Graham's political savvy. He knew a theo-political approach to spread his apocalyptic message must adapt or die, and he could not risk exclusion from the Kennedy White House.

FIVE

EVANGELICAL NATIONALISM AFTER EISENHOWER

From John F. Kennedy to Donald J. Trump

Graham's relationship to every president after Eisenhower, including Kennedy, illuminates a profound reality: Graham and other politicians came to use "under God" and the apocalyptic ideas behind it as a political totem or virtue signal to achieve certain political ends. Most presidents after Eisenhower have made it more of a cipher that politically charged figures could use to channel evangelical Christianity for personal and political gains. Yet what makes this truly shocking is that people employing these words do not know that they are reiterating and repeating Graham's opinions from decades earlier. "Under God" has truly taken on a life of its own. An examination of how presidents use "under God" shows that America never abandoned Graham's nationalistic apocalypticism; instead, evangelical Americans continue to embrace unquestioned xenophobic nationalism shaped by the ideologies and goals of sitting presidents. This means that the words Graham tried so desperately to get presidents and Americans to embrace are now used as talking points and political-spin slang to further an exceptionalist agenda.

John F. Kennedy

John F. Kennedy continued traditions like the National Prayer Breakfast and spoke at International Christian Leadership gatherings, decisions that kept Graham and other evangelicals appeased. The Cuban Missile Crisis came and left with its apocalyptic possibilities, but Graham refrained from calling out Kennedy in sermons or radio broadcasts, nor did he shout "hallelujah" at the possibility of his nation facing a fate worse than Hiroshima and Nagasaki. Despite this nuclear showdown (which Kennedy successfully negotiated a way out of), Kennedy received significant evangelical pushback following the 1962 *Vitale v. Engel* Supreme Court decision that barred official government-mandated prayer in public school settings. Kennedy's response to the decision illuminates his general approach to religion and politics, as he urges Americans to support it:

> We have in this case a very easy remedy, and that is to pray ourselves, and I would think that it would be a welcome reminder to every American family that we can pray a good deal more at home, we can attend our churches with a good deal more fidelity, and we can make the true meaning of prayer much more important in the lives of all our children.[1]

Kennedy's neutral position on the ruling fell negatively upon invigorated evangelicals. For example, a woman from Pasadena, California, penned a letter to Justice Hugo Black and used the recently amended Pledge of Allegiance with "under God" as evidence that established and confirmed that "our country was founded on faith in God."[2] Other Americans wrote to Justice Black, including some angered residents from Charlotte, North Carolina, who condemned the ruling: "Our nation has been greatly blessed 'under God,' and our motto 'in God we trust' should be emphasized in every phase of our national life."

A woman in Arizona continued the trend and wrote: "As for me and my family, we believe in the Free America, which was brought forth by our Founding Fathers—under God!"[3] These letters reflect the spread of Graham's apocalyptic, American-centric theology, as American citizens used the pledge's language to justify criticism toward a Supreme Court ruling designed to promote religious freedom, not inhibit it. They also show Americans regularly (and comfortably) employing revisionist history, as they now viewed the motto that Eisenhower added to the pledge less than ten years earlier as something that the Founding Fathers themselves created.

Lyndon Johnson

Graham never tied Kennedy's death to apocalyptic harbingers or prophetic events and, though Graham did not use the assassination as an apocalyptic sign, he was forthright after the president's death, saying in the aftermath, "I never agreed with everything he did, as most of us didn't . . . but I always liked him," and adding that Kennedy was "anxious to heal the religious breach in the country."[4] Lyndon Johnson took office, and increased popularity during the Johnson era granted Graham additional speaking and writing opportunities, prompting the publication of numerous books, many of which focused on biblical apocalypses.

Soaked in American-flavored apocalyptic devotion, Graham's *World Aflame* hit U.S. bookshelves in 1965, and the timing of the book's release was quite conspicuous given that President Johnson signed into law the Civil Rights Act in 1964 and the Voting Rights Act in 1965. Johnson marked the passage of the 1965 Voting Rights Act with a special message to Congress. The statement's conclusion recalls the pledge and Graham's American exceptionalist theology:

> Above the pyramid on the great seal of the United States it says in Latin "God has favored our undertaking." God will not favor everything that we do. It is rather our duty to divine His will. But I cannot help believing that He truly

understands and that He really favors the undertaking that
we begin here tonight.[5]

Johnson's pointed citation is intentional, as opposition to the
Voting Rights Act weaponized "under God" to support their
positions. For example, a 1964 leaflet distributed throughout
Mississippi by the Ku Klux Klan seeking new members makes
straightforward use of the language:

> We are looking for, and enlisting ONLY: Sober, Intelligent,
> Courageous, Christian, American, White men who are con-
> sciously and fully aware of the basic FACT that the physical
> life and earthly destiny are absolutely bound up with the
> Survival of this Nation, under God.[6]

Prosecutors brought this leaflet into evidence during the 1967
"Mississippi Burning" trial in which a KKK lynch mob, aided by
Mississippi police officers, abducted, beat, and murdered three
civil rights activists in the summer of 1964. The murders happened on June 21, 1964, and Johnson signed the Civil Rights Act
into law on July 2, just eleven days later. Similarly, in 1965, fundamentalist pastor Bob Jones justified his opposition to the Civil
Rights Act and the Voting Rights Act by arguing such legislation
opposed America's Christian history, and, no matter how critics
assailed him, Jones remained resilient: "Fight for the right, die
if we must, but always remember, in God we trust." Johnson's
religious language and the KKK's show the sharp differences an
image or idea can take on in different people's hands. Johnson
used the language with nuance and care, issuing a challenge to
Americans to consider their place among the cosmic structure.
Conversely, the KKK weaponized "under God" to justify murder,
racism, and terrorism. And yet, like Graham, the one thing that
both sides did was fight for their idealized America. Johnson's
America was one that considered its words and actions with considerable deference, while the Klan's America was one that bred
fear through threatening anyone and anything different.

Richard Nixon and Gerald Ford

Graham and other evangelicals rejoiced when Richard Nixon defeated Hubert Humphrey and George Wallace for president in 1968. Graham saw Nixon as the definitive Christian candidate and made that position abundantly clear in January 1968, telling Nixon, "You are the best prepared man in the United States to be president. I think it is your destiny to be president."[7] However, following the Watergate scandal, Graham grew despondent toward the president, going as far as to recall in 2011 that his experience with Nixon made him reconsider any political involvement:

> I'm grateful for the opportunities God gave me to minister to people in high places; people in power have spiritual and personal needs like everyone else, and often they have no one to talk to. But looking back I know I sometimes crossed the line, and I wouldn't do that now.[8]

When Nixon stepped down, Gerald Ford took his place for a brief but controversial presidential tenure. The efforts of the United States in Vietnam collapsed as South Vietnam fell in 1975, essentially ending the war across all fronts. American economic markets sank to numbers unseen since the Great Depression, and faith in the American governing system was now lower than it had been in decades thanks to Nixon and Watergate.

Ford, however, did not help matters when he pardoned much-maligned ex-president Nixon on September 8, 1974. His address to the nation shows he was clearly aware of the reaction that his pardon would create. Despite knowing this blowback, Ford pushes through with his choice:

> I have promised to uphold the Constitution, to do what is right as God gives me to see the right, and to do the very best that I can for America. I have asked your help and your prayers, not only when I became President but many times since. The Constitution is the supreme law of our land and it governs our actions as citizens. Only the laws of God, which govern our consciences, are superior to it. As we are a nation

under God, so I am sworn to uphold our laws with the help of God. And I have sought such guidance and searched my own conscience with special diligence to determine the right thing for me to do with respect to my predecessor in this place, Richard Nixon, and his loyal wife and family.[9]

Here Ford uses "under God" to justify pardoning a man that went from political darling to universalized adversarial figure in a matter of months. Ford bends "under God" into a divinely sanctioned instrument designed to vindicate an unfavorable presidential decision: according to Ford, it is God, not Ford, who bears ultimate responsibility for forgiveness. Thus, the phrase that Graham wielded as a global salve in the 1950s is now just another way for politicians to justify their behavior.

Ford's 1976 State of the Union address, his last as president before losing to Jimmy Carter that November, again brought Graham's apocalyptic ideology and reception to the fore. Ford, a Republican, drew considerable ire from constituents when he took steps that lessened presidential power and expanded congressional authority.[10] His 1976 State of the Union addresses these criticisms directly, echoing Graham himself in urging his audience to heed the call to accept divine control over political maneuverings:

From the opportunities which fate and my fellow citizens have given me, as a member of the House, as Vice President and President of the Senate, and as President of all the people, I have come to understand and place the highest value on the checks and balances which our founders imposed on government through the separation of powers among co-equal legislative, executive, and judicial branches. This often results in difficulty and delay, as I well know, but it also places supreme authority under God, beyond any one person, any one branch, any majority great or small, or any one party. The Constitution is the bedrock of all our freedoms. Guard and cherish it, keep honor and order in your own house, and the Republic will endure.[11]

Ford's use of "under God" here parallels his pardoning of Nixon, as Ford presents American authority as God's authority, meaning that God guides Ford's thoughts and not the other way around. And yet, his use of "under God" in both the State of the Union and the pardon announcement feels desperate, as if Ford tried to elude blame by placing culpability for his decisions upon a divine mandate that he could not escape or oppose. The tactic failed to curry national favor for Ford; he lost the election to an evangelical Baptist from Georgia. With Ford, what Graham intended for anticommunist spiritual revival now merely justified ill-advised political decisions. "Under God" was now just another political tool.

Jimmy Carter

On paper, Jimmy Carter's election looked like a homerun for Graham and evangelical American-centric ideologies. Carter hailed from the American South and grew up an active member of an evangelical congregation. Carter's homespun and genuine nature connected with working-class American voters, and his bond with individuals and communities made him more like a local pastor than a savvy politician. Despite this potential, Carter and Graham had a strained relationship. Carter was the only president during Graham's run of presidential relationships to withhold an immediate invitation to the White House, and Graham took the lack of access personally. He described their relationship with icy disappointment: "I looked at them as personal friends, not presidents, most of the time. I look on Carter as the president." Further, Graham described Carter as "very serious minded" because Graham "didn't see him much."[12] On the surface, Graham's sentiments toward Carter suggest profound respect and admiration for Carter's focus and determination. Yet read alongside Graham's previous presidential relationships, his words appear negative, even passive-aggressive. Describing Carter as the president and not as a friend underlines the alienation Graham felt from Carter, and saying that Carter and Graham saw each other sparingly is Graham's way of saying that Carter never sought Graham's insight or advice. Graham felt shut out and was unapologetic in sharing those feelings publicly.

Graham's disdain for the president aside, Carter frequently discussed his religion and faith practices but did not wear them on his sleeve, nor did he use them for political expediency like the man who would replace him, Ronald Reagan. Carter's presidency was tumultuous economically, domestically, and internationally, and he addressed such concerns on July 15, 1979, with his "Crisis of Confidence" speech. Unlike Ford's pardon of Nixon and the 1976 State of the Union address, Carter's speech is diplomatic and uses pluralistic language when referencing the Christian deity. For example, his first reference to "God" comes from an unnamed religious leader, and he couches the second reference among many factors contributing to the nation's success: "In a nation that was proud of hard work, strong families, close-knit communities, and our faith in God, too many of us now tend to worship self-indulgence and consumption." His conclusion moves closer to Graham's perspective without sacrificing Carter's textbook restraint: "With God's help and for the sake of our Nation, it is time for us to join hands in America. Let us commit ourselves together to a rebirth of the American spirit. Working together with our common faith we cannot fail."[13] Carter's language here is eerily like his relationship with Graham, in that the president mentions God only in general, nondescript terms and uses God-language with razor-like focus and not brute blunt force.

Carter eventually softened his distance from the evangelist and sought Graham's assistance with nuclear disarmament in the latter years of his presidency, but the relationship never became what Graham felt entitled to or wanted. Carter lost the 1980 presidential election to then-governor Reagan, who—with a hardline open-market economic stance, public charisma, and a renewed emphasis and vigor for making America a nation "under God"— quickly became Graham's "golden goose." This was an abrupt shift from Carter's placid religious rhetoric toward a more zealous oratory style, as Reagan made emphatic and passionate speeches about moving Christian religion front and center in a presidency defined by American exceptionalism.

Ronald Reagan

Ronald Reagan fit in well with Graham's exceptionalist apocalyptic perspective because apocalyptic American exceptionalism was old hat for the seasoned "politician" long before Reagan became president. With the conclusion of Reagan's famous 1964 "A Time for Choosing" speech (supporting Senator Barry Goldwater during Goldwater's presidential run), Reagan urges America to choose Goldwater with overt apocalyptic language that could just as easily come from Graham:

> You and I have a rendezvous with destiny. We can preserve for our children this, the last best hope of man on earth, or we can sentence them to take the first step into a thousand years of darkness. . . . There can be no security anywhere in the free world if there is not fiscal and economic stability within the United States.[14]

In a 1971 interview, Reagan shares that "the day of Armageddon isn't far off" because "Ezekiel says that fire and brimstone will be rained upon the enemies of God's people. That must mean that they'll be destroyed by nuclear weapons."[15] Further, Reagan speaks unapologetically about American's place in the divine order in his acceptance of the Republican nomination at the 1980 Republican National Convention: "It is impossible to capture in words the splendor of this vast continent which God has granted as our portion of this creation."[16]

In a move that feels like a direct response to Carter's minimal use of religious language, Reagan opens his 1981 inaugural address with a bang: "We are a nation under God, and I believe God intended for us to be free. It would be fitting and good, I think, if on each Inauguration Day in future years it should be declared a day of prayer."[17] This line set a standard that Reagan would keep during his presidency, as he regularly used divine sovereignty tied to American prosperity to propel his legislative agenda. Reagan used "under God" with such consistency and predictability that he created the current path of apocalyptic nationalism himself, making "under God" a persistent and continuing mainstay in presidential political and cultural rhetoric.

Reagan's personal diaries show that his apocalyptic xenophobia was quite genuine. An entry from 1981 discusses tensions around Syria and Saudi Arabia. The president writes, "Sometimes I wonder if we are destined to meet Armageddon."[18] Later that year, after nonchalantly discussing the weather, Reagan writes, "Got word of Israeli bombing of Iraq—nuclear reactor. I swear I believe Armageddon is near."[19] In 1983 he returns to that apocalyptic language: "Syria is poisoning the well and the possibility of an Israeli-Syrian (plus Soviet) confrontation cannot be ruled out. Armageddon in the prophecies begins with the gates of Damascus being assailed."[20] Such apocalyptic inclinations made Reagan a perfect fit for Graham's American exceptionalism, and Reagan's continued use of "under God" as president showed just how well he wielded Graham's sentiment.

Reagan stays on his apocalyptic course when he employs "under God" as evidence for a solid foundation during turbulent times in his 1982 State of the Union address: "In the face of a climate of falsehood and misinformation, we've promised the world a season of truth—the truth of our great civilized ideas: individual liberty, representative government, the rule of law under God."[21] This bold claim groups individual liberty and representative government alongside divinely ordained laws, and, in so doing, Reagan equates the universe and divine order to American freedom, government systems, and legality. He also presents America's laws as being divinely ordained, meaning that anyone opposing or rejecting those laws stands against both America and God. Further, through Reagan's lens, American laws do not need to be made into God's image because, by virtue of being American laws, they already meet God's standards.

In March 1983, in what would become known as the "Evil Empire" speech, Reagan urges his audience to reconsider and oppose any legislation that would put America at a place of "military and moral inferiority." Reagan uses "under God" twice in the speech to support his diplomatic stance and tighten the chains linking America and the Christian God. He first uses it when discussing his administration's priorities:

> I want you to know that this administration is motivated by a political philosophy that sees the greatness of America in you, her people, and in your families, churches, neighborhoods, communities—the institutions that foster and nourish values like concern for others and respect for the rule of law under God.

He employs it again when stressing what he sees as the right of every family to decide what is best for their children:

> Freedom prospers when religion is vibrant and the rule of law under God is acknowledged. When our Founding Fathers passed the first amendment, they sought to protect churches from government interference. They never intended to construct a wall of hostility between government and the concept of religious belief itself.[22]

With this speech, Reagan echoes Graham's sermons of the 1940s, 1950s, and 1960s, when the evangelist described Soviet communism as *THE* definitive cosmic anti-American evil and declared that Christian salvation could ensure American prosperity and stability. Now, through Reagan's reception, a strong, Christian-based family homelife alongside American capitalism and a strong nuclear arsenal will protect God's chosen nation.

Reagan's 1984 State of the Union address parallels his previous major public speeches when he again uses "under God" twice with Graham-like tones. He uses it first with apocalyptic echoes, and he mocks improving the world through human governments:

The problems we're overcoming are not the heritage of one person, party, or even one generation. It's just the tendency of government to grow, for practices and programs to become the nearest thing to eternal life we'll ever see on this Earth. And there's always that well-intentioned chorus of voices saying, "With a little more power and a little more money, we could do so much for the people." For a time, we forgot the American dream isn't one of making government bigger; it's keeping faith with the mighty spirit of free people under God.

Reagan builds to "under God" with claims of government overreach as the enemy of the American dream. This "mighty spirit of free people," not human bureaucracy, is essential for global stability. The president's words may as well come from Graham himself, as faith in God and country, not governments, reigns supreme. The second use recalls Reagan's 1983 State of the Union address when he makes government-sanctioned school prayer his political lightning rod and invokes "under God" to address it:

And while I'm on this subject, each day your members observe a 200-year-old tradition meant to signify America is one nation under God. I must ask: If you can begin your day with a member of the clergy standing right here leading you in prayer, then why can't freedom to acknowledge God be enjoyed again by children in every schoolroom across this land?[23]

Here again, in a theologically and politically savvy move, Reagan makes his political stance overtly theological to ask why children lack the same privilege of praying that elected officials enjoy daily. One cannot deny Reagan's strategy here, as the Supreme Court ruling against which he continuously rails does not eliminate voluntary school prayer; rather, the ruling prohibits paid employees of the government from leading prayer in government-funded spaces.[24] Despite the legal niceties, Reagan withholds entertaining such distinctions in back-to-back State of the Union addresses that use "under God" to besmirch a complex Supreme

Court ruling meant to protect religious freedom. This move galvanized and appeased his base, effectively doubling down on his newfound "America under God or else" platform.

Beyond State of the Union addresses, Reagan consistently employed "under God" on national stages for political gain and to appease his voting base. For example, Reagan accepted the Republican Party's nomination for president on August 23, 1984, by further equating "under God" with foundational American ideals, without which the nation itself could not stand:

> We don't celebrate dependence day on the Fourth of July. We celebrate Independence Day. We celebrate the right of each individual to be recognized as unique, possessed of dignity and the sacred right to life, liberty, and the pursuit of happiness. At the same time, with our independence goes a generosity of spirit more evident here than in almost any other part of the world. Recognizing the equality of all men and women, we're willing and able to lift the weak, cradle those who hurt, and nurture the bonds that tie us together as one nation under God.[25]

Reagan presents America and everything it stands for as a flowing through "under God" and argues that government-centric economic systems limit individual liberty and lead to totalitarianism. He also echoes those letters written to Justice Black in the 1960s, as he conflates "life, liberty, and the pursuit of happiness" with "one nation under God," making it appear as though the two phrases come from the Declaration of Independence and are interchangeable.

President Reagan gave a rousing speech at a 1984 Ecumenical Prayer Breakfast in Dallas. Here, he presents the need for religious morality and a return to the religiosity of the nation's "Founding Fathers and Mothers." Reagan's speech touches more than once on patriotic bedrock, as he invokes George Washington, James Madison, and John F. Kennedy alongside a conflation of the Mayflower Compact and the Declaration of Independence. True to his political base, Reagan also speaks negatively about 1960s countercultural movements and what he calls "steps toward secularizing our nation and removing religion from its honored place." The speech ends with an American-centric theological position soaked in Graham-flavored apocalyptic ideology: "And without God, democracy will not and cannot long endure. If we ever forget that we're one nation under God, then we will be a nation gone under."[26]

Everything in this speech builds to this "nation gone under" sentence, preparing the way with lines like "the more decent the citizens, the more decent the state" and "only those humble enough to admit they're sinners can bring to democracy the tolerance it requires in order to survive." Reagan also brilliantly orients his American-focused view to this ecumenical audience by interchanging "religion" with "God" and presenting "one nation under God" as ecumenical, effectively smoothing Graham's apocalyptic Christian rhetoric into something more palatable and less vitriolic. He stresses to his audience that religion is the key to both American and global success:

> We establish no religion in this country, nor will we ever. We command no worship. We mandate no belief. But we poison our society when we remove its theological underpinnings. We court corruption when we leave it bereft of belief. All are free to believe or not believe; all are free to practice a faith or not. But those who believe must be free to speak of and act on their belief, to apply moral teaching to public questions. I submit to you that the tolerant society is open to and encouraging of all religions. And this does not weaken us; it strengthens us, it makes us strong. You know, if we look back through history to all those great civilizations, those great nations that rose up to even world dominance and then deteriorated, declined, and fell, we find they all had one thing in common. One of the significant forerunners of their fall was their turning away from their God or gods.[27]

Reagan's religious language is both cautionary and appealing as he makes "under God" the cure that can realign the worldwide political sphere. Simply turning to God ensures global economic and social prosperity.

Reagan's 1984 presidential victory surprised no one, and his second inaugural address, on January 21, 1985, showed that Reagan's final presidential term would look just like his first. He uses "under God" twice during the speech but separates the phrase from "one nation," instead opting to say Americans are "one people under God." His first iteration commends economic growth, saying that, as "one people under God," the nation is "determined that our future shall be worthy of our past." He then closes with an impassioned theological cry for unity under God:

> We raise our voices to the God who is the Author of this most tender music.[28] And may He continue to hold us close as we fill the world with our sound—in unity, affection, and love—one people under God, dedicated to the dream of freedom that He has placed in the human heart, called upon now to pass that dream on to a waiting and hopeful world.[29]

This connects America with divine favor in a shockingly overt fashion. His call to the nation to "raise our voices" to a God that he calls "the Author of this most tender music" ties the fate of his presidential tenure to God's divine cosmological plan. To Reagan, American freedom is divine freedom, meaning that opposing such freedom opposes the God that created (and can destroy) everything.

Reagan boldly declares at the 1985 State of the Union address, "Our progress began not in Washington, D.C., but in the hearts of our families, communities, workplaces, and voluntary groups which, together, are unleashing the invincible spirit of one great nation under God."[30] His 1986 State of the Union address follows a similar path when Reagan again credits American prosperity to this specific divine orientation: "What brought America back? The American people brought us back with quiet courage and common sense, with undying faith that in this nation under God the future will be ours; for the future belongs to the free."[31] Reagan speaks frankly and with considerable clarity: the nation is on the brink of destruction (despite his previous four-year presidential tenure) and can save itself only by submitting to God.

The last time Reagan used "under God" in a major speech was on August 15, 1988, in his farewell address at the Republican National Convention:

> We have pretty strong notions that higher tax receipts are no inherent right of the Federal Government. We don't think that inflation and high interest rates show compassion for the poor, the young, and the elderly. We respect the values that bind us together as families and as a nation. For our children, we don't think it's wrong to have them committed to pledging each day to the "one nation, under God, indivisible, with liberty and justice for all." And we have so many requirements in their classrooms; why can't we at least have one thing that is, voluntary, and that is allow our kids to repair quietly to their faith to say a prayer to start the day, as Congress does. For the unborn, quite simply, shouldn't they be able to live to become children in those classrooms?[32]

Reagan never uttered the phrase before an intentionally global audience or outside the United States, nor did he use it with smaller, less public speeches. He used "under God" only when he knew a large American audience would hear it, and the excerpt from his RNC send-off is emblematic of how and why he took that approach. Like Graham, Reagan knew his audience and played to it, meaning that he took every chance to speak before large assemblies as an opportunity to spread his American-centric political theology. Reagan consistently associated robust economic seasons with a Graham-tinged patriotic theological lens, and he framed American success around the idea that following God can only yield prosperity. Denying God will only lead to American—and, in turn, global—despair. And yet, despite adamant use of "under God" as a foundational element of America's history, Reagan's apparent ignorance of the recent inclusion of "under God" into the national rhetorical climate shows how easily and quickly one reception becomes standard. Perhaps most importantly, he invoked the phrase so often and with such vigor that, because of Reagan's presidency, "under

God" is now a staple that evangelical Christians look and listen for in the life and works of current presidents. Reagan made it a standard that impassioned evangelicals and indifferent Christians alike use to measure presidential success or failure.

George H. W. Bush

Like Carter, President George H. W. Bush initially carried his religious background in an unassuming manner by keeping faith matters strategic without sacrificing political opportunity. However, as a presidential candidate, his religious preferences were quite different. During an interview with Roger Sherman from the American Atheists, H. W. Bush declared, "I don't know that Atheists should be considered as citizens, nor should they be considered patriots. This is one nation under God."[33] Though the interview received minimal circulation, pushback was enough to make H. W. Bush change how he approached "under God" language and religion in general. He then took a much less aggressive approach, preferring to studiously avoid ruffling the feathers of evangelical voters.

Unlike Reagan, Bush did not say "under God" at his RNC acceptance speech or inauguration. The only time he used it in a formal public setting during his presidential run was on September 25, 1988, during a debate with Democratic presidential nominee Michael Dukakis. He broached the subject during a discussion about Dukakis' ACLU affiliation, saying that "under God" deserves to be on American currency in the same way that the Catholic Church should receive tax exemptions and child pornography should be illegal. This minimalist approach makes "under God" so commonsensical that, according to Bush's logic, opposing it would be akin to supporting child pornography.

H. W. Bush played well to his audience but remained wary of open religiosity. For example, consider his State of the Union address on January 31, 1990:

> And, parents, your children look to you for direction and guidance. Tell them of faith and family. Tell them we are one

nation under God. Teach them that of all the many gifts they
can receive liberty is their most precious legacy, and of all
the gifts they can give the greatest is helping others.[34]

Now "under God" is something that parents should teach their
children, as Bush combined it with family, liberty, and good citizenship. Such rhetorical softening reflected his overall approach
to theologizing American political ideas, as he dispensed with
the key phrase in his 1991 and 1992 State of the Union addresses
and when he accepted his party's presidential nomination at the
1992 Republican National Convention.

H. W. Bush believed that "under God" rhetoric was important, but, unlike Reagan, he saw the American people as the real
"god" he felt compelled to appease. American evangelical Christians rose to national and economic prominence during the
Reagan era and still held visible influence during H. W. Bush's
presidency. Thus, if a president failed to check the "under God"
box, evangelicals made their sentiments and anger known.
H. W. Bush never decried the phrase, but he also never made
it his political cross to bear. One can only speculate about how
and why he pulled back from something Reagan held so dear,
but changing global political and social tides foreshadowed the
fall of Soviet communism, meaning that Graham and other
like-minded evangelicals would have to find another apocalyptic bogeyman threatening American stability.

Bill Clinton

Compared to Reagan and H. W. Bush, Bill Clinton spoke softly
about religion, preferring to prioritize policy over religiosity.
He was, however, unapologetically Christian and even claimed
to have been "born again."[35] He navigated theo-political waters
with considerable skill by speaking at National Prayer Breakfasts,
seeking advice from Graham, and taking to the pulpit at many
predominantly black Christian churches. Despite these public
professions of faith, however, Clinton failed to appease evangelical voters, as his scandals and missteps, however in line with

previous "presidential" conduct, placed the forty-second president last in moral authority among evangelical voters.[36]

With one exception, Clinton never used "under God" in any major speeches, including both inauguration speeches and every State of the Union address. The only time Clinton used the phrase in a major public speech was on January 27, 2000, with his final State of the Union address. Then, he wove a tapestry of hope grounded in tangible change, wanting to move past his missteps boldly into the twenty-first century, painting a picture of a nation heading into the new millennium:

> To 21st century America, let us pledge these things: Every child will begin school ready to learn and graduate ready to succeed. Every family will be able to succeed at home and at work, and no child will be raised in poverty. We will meet the challenge of the aging of America. We will assure quality, affordable health care, at last, for all Americans. We will make America the safest big country on Earth. We will pay off our national debt for the first time since 1835. We will bring prosperity to every American community. We will reverse the course of climate change and leave a safer, cleaner planet. America will lead the world toward shared peace and prosperity and the far frontiers of science and technology. And we will become at last what our Founders pledged us to be so long ago: *One nation, under God, indivisible, with liberty and justice for all.* These are great goals, worthy of a great nation.[37]

Clinton shows the impact of Reagan's reception, as he associates the origin of "one nation under God" with America's Founding Fathers and nothing else. According to Clinton's reception, these words were not merely signed into law with Eisenhower's 1954 legislation; they were spoken over two hundred years ago by the Founding Fathers themselves. This is a peculiar oversight by the usually studious and fastidious Clinton, as he was known for personally revising speeches. Thus, the claim that America's founders coined "one nation under God" is a direct reflection of Reagan. Because of Reagan, Graham's apocalyptic ideology is such

an ingrained part of the shared American cultural conscious-
ness that Clinton used this revisionist history without a second
thought.

George W. Bush

George W. Bush's presidency continued the trend set by Clinton,
as his inaugural address and first State of the Union address came
up empty, making it seem like "under God" had lost any political
or public bite. Even the attacks on New York City on September 11, 2001, could not compel him to use it. And yet, in 2002,
in the small town of Ripley, West Virginia, George W. Bush reas-
sured a small crowd celebrating the Fourth of July: "No authority of government can ever prevent an American from pledging
allegiance to this one nation under God. Once again, history has
called America to use our overwhelming power in the defense of
freedom and we'll do just that."[38] Bush's words came in response
to a 2002 California ruling that deemed "under God" in violation
of the Establishment Clause of the First Amendment.[39] W. Bush
was like Reagan with his support of something that faced no real
threat, and calling attention to school prayer only bolstered his
standing among potential evangelical voters without making any
measurable change.

With the Pledge of Allegiance Reaffirmation Act, on November 13, 2002, President W. Bush also made a bold statement on the
power of the evangelical voter and the nation's (fabricated) connection to "one nation under God." W. Bush signed this performative
bill to confirm "one Nation under God" in the Pledge of Allegiance,
and "In God We Trust" as the national motto of the United States.
Language in the bill extended beyond what Reagan solidified and
Clinton continued, saying that the pilgrims themselves sailed on
November 11, 1620 with a sentiment akin to "one nation under
God" in their hearts, while also tying the Mayflower Compact to the
phrase with shocking directness.[40] According to this bill, "one nation
under God" lies behind the very spirit of the First Amendment and
even American religious freedom despite similar legislation from

Eisenhower showing the very origin of the phrase's implementation into the Pledge of Allegiance. As with his response in West Virginia, at no point leading up to his signing of the bill did either "under God" or "In God We Trust" face any viable threat.

Barack Obama

Obama's presidency marked the unique evolution of Graham's reception as his use of "under God" confirmed that Reagan's reception endured as the unquestioned standard. Critics assailed Obama's religious beliefs early in his 2008 presidential campaign, and, despite public support from Christian organizations and his pastor, many detractors, including future president Donald Trump, claimed President Obama was actually a Muslim. Undeterred by such criticisms, Obama used "under God" in only two major speeches. The first came on May 1, 2011, with his remarks on the death of Osama bin Laden. He shared the news with American citizens and urged a spirit of national unity, saying that bin Laden's death concluded a national effort begun nearly a decade earlier:

> That is the story of our history, whether it's the pursuit of prosperity for our people, or the struggle for equality for all our citizens; our commitment to stand up for our values abroad, and our sacrifices to make the world a safer place. Let us remember that we can do these things not just because of wealth or power, but because of who we are: one nation, under God, indivisible, with liberty and justice for all.[41]

Obama used it again on September 8, 2011, in an address to Congress on the American Jobs Act:

> No single individual built America on their own. We built it together. We have been, and always will be, one nation, under God, indivisible, with liberty and justice for all; a nation with responsibilities to ourselves and with responsibilities to one another. And members of Congress, it is time for us to meet our responsibilities.[42]

Obama's scant and calculated use of "under God" represents his presidential religiosity, as he regularly downplayed religious affiliation, much like President Carter, in favor of areligious legislation.

Opponents noticed Obama's approach to religion, and the 2012 election brought Obama under further religious scrutiny. Republican candidate Mitt Romney pressed Obama by making "under God" part of his devoutly religious election platform. Romney spoke at the Military Aviation Museum in Virginia Beach and attacked Obama with the Pledge of Allegiance:

> That pledge says "under God." I will not take "God" out of the name of our platform. I will not take "God" off our coins, and I will not take God out of my heart. We're a nation bestowed by God.[43]

Using the pledge as a campaign talking point is a twofold move for Romney. First, he assails Obama by prompting his audience to recall opposition toward Obama's religion and unsubstantiated claims toward the president being a secret Muslim. Second, Romney echoes Reagan and his insistence on making "under God" a personal and national priority, despite no one threatening to remove "under God" during Obama's presidency.

Discussion around Obama and "under God" peaked in 2013 when critics accused President Obama of omitting the phrase from Abraham Lincoln's "Gettysburg Address." People expressed great outrage through social media outlets when Obama, among many other prominent voices, participated in a Ken Burns documentary special about Lincoln's most famous speech and its effect on the Civil War and, in turn, American history. The president drew ire for not including "under God" in his recitation, with some critics claiming he eliminated the line on purpose, thereby proving his religious illegitimacy.[44] Lincoln's famous speech does include "under God," but controversy surrounds its very inclusion. Lincoln's address exists in two primary versions: the Hay copy and the Bliss copy. The Bliss version includes "under God," but many scholars and experts lobby for the Hay version as the original, arguing that someone amended the Bliss copy by adding "under God" for posterity. Such discussion around Obama's choice to use the Hay copy over the Bliss shows the complete retrojection of Graham's reception and Reagan's perfection of "under God" as a political totem onto the American psyche. Experts legitimately do not know if Lincoln uttered "under God" that fateful day in Gettysburg, but Americans accept "under God" as so essential that anyone saying otherwise is wrong—un-American and disgraceful.

Donald J. Trump

Many things could define Donald Trump's presidency, but something truly remarkable and exceedingly relevant to Graham's apocalyptic worldview is how the forty-fifth president used the cultural union of America and evangelical Christianity to his advantage. Trump took much from Reagan's political playbook, including Reagan's evangelical fervor, through similar strategies with comparable results, as his speeches were calculated tools designed to energize his voting base. Trump's campaign lifted the "Make America Great Again" slogan from Reagan's 1980 presidential campaign slogan, "Let's make America great again." Like Reagan, Trump ran a simple but direct campaign that vowed to undo decisions made by a preceding Democratic president. Trump also made religious rhetoric essential to his public platform, as he used "under God" to support his views of religious freedom and a pro-life stance on abortion.

Controversy followed Trump as he began his presidential run with a galvanizing speech laced with polarizing rhetoric, a move that separated him from Republican competitors in the months before the 2016 presidential election. Trump ran on an anti-Obama, pro-America platform that presented the Obama era like an apocalyptic nightmare that brought America to the brink of annihilation. At a September 2016 Values Voter Summit in Washington, D.C., Trump came on stage with his Bible and started blazing an America-under-God trail that he would continue through his election victory: "Imagine what our country could accomplish if we started working together as one people, under one God, saluting one flag."[45] Trump used that line in campaign rallies at different locations across key states, including Iowa, Pennsylvania, and North Carolina, which proved to be a politically savvy move, as Trump won all three of those states in an upset victory over Democratic nominee Hillary Clinton.[46]

The use of the phrase with the new and savvy emphasis on "one God"—and the shift to "one people, under one God"— narrowed the reception and underlined its monotheistic roots. Press and media members reacted to Trump's adjustment with surprise and uncertainty, claiming that the move alienated Hindu, atheist, and First Nations American voters, as their faiths and practices are not monotheistic. Trump's move was indeed a bold one, but it had precedence in roots planted by Graham and cultivated by previous presidents—adding "one" only solidified what was already in place. Graham's cries for national revival and Eisenhower's legislation were not mindful of non-monotheistic faiths, nor did they incorporate monotheistic faiths outside Judaism and Christianity. Trump himself expressed anti-Muslim sentiment on more than one occasion, and his expansion of "under God" to "under one God" may be seen as a hardline articulation of ongoing Islamophobic sentiment among his voting base.[47] Using the phrase and changing it to reflect what his voters wanted to hear was a calculated and intentional move, as he continued Reagan's repetitive implementation while injecting his rhetoric so subtly that supporters barely noticed and approved without question.

Trump returned to the traditional rhetoric of "one nation under God" during his 2017 and 2018 National Prayer Breakfast addresses but included an additional layer to his reception during the Christmas holiday seasons. On December 9, 2017, he wrote on Twitter, "We believe that every American should stand for the National Anthem, and we proudly pledge allegiance to one NATION UNDER GOD!"[48] Included with the text was a campaign rally picture with "Merry Christmas" signs mixed among general pro-Trump signage. Adding to this, Trump spoke during the 2018 National Day of Prayer and claimed an outright victory because, according to his unsupported claims, more Americans were saying "under God" and "Merry Christmas" with greater frequency since his election.[49] Trump took the phrase, stripped it of any possible nuance, and made it an outright political pawn that he used at will to placate his voting base and promote his "America First" platform. Further, by including that Americans should "stand for the National Anthem," Trump crossed off another item on his rhetorical junket, as the "stand" language refers to NFL and NCAA athletes choosing to kneel during pregame national anthem ceremonies to protest American police brutality against black people and other minoritized persons. Trump vocally opposed such protests early and often in his presidency, which prompted more protesting against the president's calls for owners to, as he put it, "get that son of a bitch off the field" when a player knelt during the anthem.[50]

Trump eventually conflated the pledge, the national anthem, and "under God" into a reusable political totem that he happily employed as needed. One such occasion was a speech at the Veterans of Foreign Wars National Convention on July 24, 2018. Here, he addresses the crowd and pays homage to American freedom, the flag, and one nation under God:

> To every single member of the VFW, because of your service, your courage, and your example, we are restoring the dreams and the glory, and the greatness of America. We will never give in. We will never give up. And we will never stop fighting for our country, our flag, and our freedom. Together we will keep on fighting and we will keep on winning as one people, one family, and one nation under God. Thank you. God bless you. God bless our veterans. And God bless the United States of America. Thank you very much.[51]

At a January 2020 "Evangelicals for Trump" rally, an assembly of evangelical leaders gathered around the president, laid hands on him, and prayed over him as the emcee urged the audience to "extend hands" with them, with one pastor praying words that sounded step-for-step like something Graham would have preached in the 1940s: "Heavenly Father, we come to you today and we thank you for this nation that was born in 1776. We pray in 2020 that it would be born again."[52] Also, like Graham, Trump argued that saying "under God" is as important as believing it. For example, on May 3, 2018, on a self-proclaimed National Day of Prayer, Trump addressed an eager crowd at the White House:

> It uplifts the soul, inspires action, and unites us all as one nation, under God. So important. And we say it here. You know, a lot of people—[applause]—they don't say it. But you know what? They're starting to say it more. Just like we're starting to say, "Merry Christmas" when that day comes around. [Applause.] You notice the big difference between now and two or three years ago? It was—Paula, it was going in the other direction rapidly. Right? Now it's straight up.[53]

Trump's reception of "one nation under God" embodied the political and social factors that Graham preached in the 1940s and 1950s, but without Graham's sense of moral fortitude. Graham fought hard for people to make changes in personal and communal morality to ensure the nation's place under God, but Trump appeared satisfied with simply saying the words without measurable moral and ethical changes.

Another preeminent example of Trump's reception in action came during the 2019 State of the Union address:

> We must keep America first in our hearts. We must keep freedom alive in our souls. And we must always keep faith in America's destiny—that one Nation, under God, must be the hope and the promise and the light and the glory among all the nations of the world![54]

Graham urged leaders throughout his career to make America a godly nation in both word and deed, and, with his State of the Union address, Trump followed a similar path and attempted to convince the nation that God is preeminent. Despite Trump's religious rhetoric, his lifestyle choices before he became president, his language toward women and members of ethnic and sexual minorities, and his political obstinacy in the face of opposition bore little resemblance to the conservative religious utopia Graham envisioned. For Trump and his base, it was enough to use the phrase and stop there.

No other president, not even Reagan, rode "under God" with such dramatic flair as Trump, and none has been so quick to readjust the evangelical morality tied to it. Further, the willingness of certain evangelicals to align with Trump shows how flexible their religious conscience can be when given a seat at the proverbial table. Consistent use of the phrase in Trump's speeches and rallies shows that he knew its power, and he returned to it with razor-like precision. For example, the Trump White House released a "fact sheet," presented as news, showing how "President Donald J. Trump Stands Up for Religious Freedom in the United States." One heading reads, "ONE NATION UNDER GOD: President Trump has publicly stood with people of faith and with those who advocate for the sanctity of life." Words beneath the heading, which the sheet again presents as facts, include Trump's National Prayer Breakfast attendance, multiple declarations for national days of prayer, speaking at the Value Voters Summit, and becoming the first president to attend the annual anti-abortion March for Life.[55] Each of these "facts" is a clear political talking point designed to bolster Trump's resume, as church attendance continued to decline throughout his presidency and more Americans moved away from organized religion with each passing year. Graham worked with words to inspire a cultural revolution, one fueled by a profound sense of apocalyptic urgency; with Trump, Graham's words and ideas now changed according to whatever the political moment required.

Conclusion

Words are, by their very nature, tools created by people for people to use. How people use those words depends on who they are and what goals they have in mind. The purpose of this study has been to show how an idea can start in one place and, through the power of words and personal will, can end up somewhere completely unintended and unforeseen. When Billy Graham began preaching and teaching an apocalyptic gospel for America in the 1940s, he urged Americans to become a nation under God or else the world would suffer and possibly end. Graham rode that belief and those words into some of the biggest and most powerful halls that the world had to offer, and as his popularity grew so too did the influence of his words. Graham's reach exceeded his grasp, however, and others like George Docherty took it upon themselves to carry that national-theological torch, which led to Eisenhower's forging of Graham's beliefs into the national motto. From there, the concept of a nation "under God" ceased to belong to anyone. Rather, it took on a life of its own, with succeeding presidents determining how they employ (or shun) those words according to their own political ends.

The path that began with Graham and that lives on through President Trump is far from unique; ideas and words frequently lose all traces of their original meaning in favor of the here and now. However, what makes Graham's apocalyptic worldview remarkable is the life it now has as a political cipher. Presidents and elected officials point to "under God" as a bedrock and foundational idea that came with the earliest British settlers. This interpretation of the pledge exists because people in power made that claim, despite historical evidence to the contrary. Even then, knowing the date of legislation tells but a fraction of the story: the seeds of that motto lie in the apocalyptic hopes and dreams of one man, which themselves began in the sermons, writings, and teachings that came before him. No idea is ever truly dead, and no interpretation is ever permanent. The belief that America is a divinely chosen nation upon which all humanity depends has taken many paths, but its future lies in the hands of people wielding this idea for political, social, and cultural gain.

CONCLUSION

With Liberty and Justice for Some

Like Father, Like Son

On June 1, 2020, President Donald Trump took an early evening walk. It was a clear evening with favorable weather, though meteorologists noted it was a touch hot with little wind. This made the tear gas that Trump ordered upon peaceful protestors outside the White House hang in the air a bit more, prompting those peaceful protestors to flee for cover. Thousands were out protesting the murder of George Floyd, a black man from Minneapolis, and the president wanted to respond in a way that reflected his priorities and values. Trump walked up to the St. John's Episcopal Church uninvited, and, after police forcibly removed a visiting priest and seminary student distributing water and supplies to people who may have needed them, Trump held up a Bible and stood for a photo op.[1] Video shows the president standing with the Bible by the right side of his head, and as sirens blare in the background against the sound of police firing even more tear gas farther away, someone asked, "Is that your Bible?" The president responded, "It's a Bible."[2]

Later that night on CNN, Bishop Mariann Edgar Budde of the Episcopal Diocese of Washington spoke about Trump's actions and decried everything the president did leading up to the event, during the photo shoot, and in the aftermath. Bishop Budde spoke with CNN's Anderson Cooper:

> I am outraged. The President did not pray when he came to St. John's, nor as you just articulated, did he acknowledge the agony of our country right now, and in particular, that of the people of color in our nation, who wonder if any-one ever—anyone in public power will ever acknowledge their sacred words. And who are rightfully demanding an end to 400 years of systemic racism and white supremacy in our country. And I just want the world to know, that we in the diocese of Washington, following Jesus and his way of love . . . we distance ourselves from the incendiary language of this President. We follow someone who lived a life of nonviolence and sacrificial love. We align ourselves with those seeking justice for the death of George Floyd and countless others. And I just can't believe what my eyes have seen.[3]

Contrasting Bishop Budde's palpable anger, Graham's son (and president/CEO of the Billy Graham Evangelical Association), Franklin Graham, responded via Twitter on June 2, 2020, at 9:09 a.m. with an accompanying picture of Trump holding the Bible: "Yesterday @POTUS Trump made a statement by walk-ing to @StJohnLafayette that had been vandalized & set on fire in Sunday night's riot. God & His Word are the only hope for our nation."[4] The younger Graham included a link to a *New York Post* article that discusses Trump's invocation of the Insurrection Act of 1807 that allowed him to use military force in response to nationwide protests.

The respective responses of the bishop and of Franklin Graham show that Billy Graham's "one nation under God" legacy endures, as one Christian leader reacted with horror and outrage over the president's actions, but another took the response and the accompanying military force as signs of Trump's strength as a Christian leader. Trump did not even have to say, "We are a nation under God," for his supporters and evangelicals to hear it; all he had to do was hold a Bible and stand. Prominent evangelical leader and chairman of the Faith and Freedom Coalition Ralph Reed expressed similar praise for Trump's tactic: "His presence sent the twin message that our streets and cities do not belong to rioters and domestic terrorists, and that the ultimate answer to what ails our country can be found in the repentance, redemption, and forgiveness of the Christian faith."[5] For Franklin Graham and other evangelicals, a strong president is one that holds a Bible in one hand and the nation's military in the other, despite the likely disingenuous nature of Trump's political theater stunt in a time of national unrest.

Franklin's response to Trump matches the younger Graham's theo-political sentiment around the forty-fifth president, as he readily uses apocalyptic language that may as well have come from Billy Graham himself. However, unlike his father, Franklin speaks without any sense of subtlety regarding his political agenda. For example, on November 26, 2019, Franklin spoke with Texas evangelist and radio host Eric Metaxas on Metaxas' syndicated radio show. Metaxas talked plainly and with candor when asking Franklin about President Donald Trump: "What do you think of what is happening now? I mean, it's a very bizarre situation to be living in a country where some people seem to exist to undermine the president of the United States. It's just a bizarre time for most Americans."[6] Franklin responded earnestly, "Well, I believe it's almost a demonic power that is trying—" at which Metaxas interrupted and built upon Graham's point before he could finish: "I would disagree. It's not almost demonic. You know and I know, at the heart, it's a spiritual battle."[7] Despite his initial appraisal of anti-Trump sentiment being "demonic," the younger Graham backtracked in response to Metaxas' nuance, arguing that Trump's robust economy lead to greater opportunities for individuals to tithe and thereby improve the greater

Christian church worldwide. Metaxas kept the conversation focused on people taking an anti-Trump position:

> People seem to have devolved to a kind of moralistic Phar-isaism, and they say, "How can you support somebody blah, blah, blah," and then go on to cite how he's the least Christ—you know, they go on and on, and I think these people don't, they don't even have a biblical view when it comes to that—you know, that if somebody doesn't hold to our theology, that doesn't mean they can't be a great pilot, or a great doctor or dentist. I mean, it's a bizarre situation that we're in, that people seem only to have standards for the president somehow.[8]

Emboldened and encouraged by Metaxas, Graham narrowed his focus to articulate his point: "I believe that Donald Trump believes—he believes in God. He believes in Jesus Christ. His depth—he doesn't, you know, he went to churches here in New York; he didn't get a whole lot of teaching."[9]

Media outlets erupted, with some favoring Graham's sentiment and others decrying the evangelical leader's words. However, scoffers and supports alike failed to hear Franklin echoing his father's political sentiments, as Franklin's statements are spun from his father's theo-political cloth, from which was spun the very language that prompted President Eisenhower's decision to mandate the inclusion of "under God" in the pledge over sixty years ago. Franklin continues his father's apocalyptic influence, as he justifies the political work of Donald Trump, a man whose words, choices, and deeds regularly oppose the evangelical doctrine that Franklin lobbies so hard to nationalize and legislate. Franklin overlooks glaring inconsistencies between what he and Trump respectively believe and does so simply because Trump presents a "godly" facade, which, ironically, goes to the heart of what the elder Graham preached about and warned against in the 1940s.

But what Franklin seems to neglect is his father's clear change of heart following disappointments and misdirections from political leaders, as Franklin is comfortable aligning with Trump because of Trump's national power and status. It seems that if Trump does the bare minimum and publicly adheres to a vague form of Christianity, Franklin believes America and, in turn, the world are on the right spiritual path. Franklin's appraisal and support of Trump stands in stark contrast to his disdain for President Obama. Like his father's comparisons between Carter and Reagan, Franklin sees Obama as spiritually weak and has repeatedly argued that the forty-fourth president is indeed a Muslim. For example, in 2010, Franklin declared:

> I think the president's problem is that he was born a Muslim; his father was a Muslim. The seed of Islam is passed through the father like the seed of Judaism is passed through the mother. He was born a Muslim, his father gave him an Islamic name. Now it's obvious that the president has renounced the prophet Mohammed, and he has renounced Islam, and he has accepted Jesus Christ. That's what he says he has done. I cannot say that he hasn't. So I just have to believe that the president is what he has said.[10]

Franklin added to this position in 2011, claiming without evidence that Obama's religion was allowing the Muslim Brotherhood to infiltrate the American government. Franklin later apologized for his remarks about Obama's faith, however disingenuously, in a 2012 letter to NAACP faith leaders, saying that "the president has said he is a Christian and I accept that." Franklin readily disagreed with Obama's foreign, domestic, and economic policies but believes in President Trump because of Trump's "America First" platforms, despite outcries from fellow Christian and evangelical leaders. He still only says what is necessary to avoid public-relations blowback about President Obama, showing that his father's apocalyptic legacy lives on through his son, his politics, and the millions of people who follow and trust Franklin for spiritual guidance. All it takes to earn Franklin's trust is to claim America is "one nation under God." Here is a radical, and ironic, shift: a Graham (Billy) originally espoused this vision of America, and now a Graham (Franklin) readily receives this vision as a sign of divine presidential authenticity.[11]

On the surface, Franklin's behavior seems incongruous to the elder Graham's stance on Christian leadership, but the analysis of Graham's apocalyptic nationalism here shows quite the opposite as Franklin situates himself within a long line of Christian interpreters that insert themselves into global political affairs. Franklin builds upon his father's work and shows that nothing people make or create remains truly "theirs." Franklin uses his father's legacy to build his own while reconstructing his father's political and theological positions on religion and government. And yet, it is Billy Graham's very American-centric ideas that pave the way for Franklin's success and access, creating interpretive continuity between the evangelist and his son. Franklin is truly his father's son, but, unlike Billy, Franklin starts with a seat at the tables of power, a place that leaves ample room for unabashed support for Trump and that puts him in the company of like-minded evangelicals working to remake America in their image.

Predicting What Is Next

A cursory internet search for "Under God in Daniel" or "Under God in Revelation" yields millions of Google hits, including links to sites with titles containing some form (or combination) of "The End Times," "Unlocking the Code," and "Rapture Ready."[12] Greater access to ideas and tools across the internet keeps the wheels of apocalyptic reception spinning ever faster. Further, each site, opinion, reflection, and exegesis carries a clear evangelical Christian bent with discussions framing Daniel and Revelation as crucial to understanding the modern era.

Billy Graham himself now takes on a second life of sorts online, with full access to sermons and interviews allowing future generations to hear the evangelist for the first time. BillyGraham .org allows the visitor to leave 24/7 prayer requests that someone from the Billy Graham Evangelistic Association will read and respond to, making the visitor feel like Graham still lives just a click away. Sermons curated for the current political moment line the homepage, with the latest news from Franklin Graham dotting the margins. Billy Graham's spirit has become a wellspring for evangelical pasturage, as supporters handpick his words to support the warm, cuddly reconstruction of a man sparked by divine conviction. But what is lost among current amateur apocalypticism and Graham's internet fame is the crucial role Graham played in normalizing something as radically xenophobic as American apocalyptic thought. Graham genuinely believed that "under God" would become a protective barrier that would insulate the United States and, in turn, the world from encroaching forms of satanic evil. Now presidents use the phrase to keep zealous voters with access to the internet happy and ready to support them.

And so we must grapple with the reality of interpretations and what they can become. Graham never intended for white supremacists to take his "under God" idea and use it to justify their bigoted sense of America, but Graham also wedded himself to ideas of American exceptionalism and the problematic theology that comes with them. This is the very nature of any idea, especially a biblical interpretation: that what one creates can become something else entirely when it leaves one's hands. Try as we might, we cannot control the destiny of our work, and in the case of Graham it seems his plans have backfired, as "under God" now reinforces a narrow understanding of what America is, and failure to comply with that "America" leads to division, anger, and dissent. Graham took a significant risk in gambling so much of his theology on apocalypticism, and now the destruction that he fought so hard to stop eats the nation from within.

Herein lies the possible future of apocalyptic thought and how people use it. As the biblical books of Daniel and Revelation were written so many years ago to warn their audiences about the dangers of unchecked political power and misplaced priorities, Graham's method of interpretation itself is now a warning that echoes throughout history and urges people to consider whom they serve and under what flag they kneel. Despite his body having long been buried, Graham's ideas and interpretations are far from dead, which underlines the need to doggedly pursue the question of "Who, what, why, and for how much?" anytime someone says, "The Bible tells me so . . ."

NOTES

INTRODUCTION

1 Aleanna Siacon, "Rep. Rashida Tlaib Slams North Carolina Gun Billboard for 'Inciting Violence,'" *Asheville Citizen-Times*, July 31, 2019.

2 Edward Helmore, "'How Is This Not Inciting Violence?': Gun Shop Billboard Targets the 'Squad,'" *Guardian*, August 1, 2019.

3 Grant Wacker, *America's Pastor* (Cambridge, Mass.: Harvard University Press, 2014).

4 Cathy Lynn Grossman, "Billy Graham, America's Pastor, Has Died," *USA Today*, February 21, 2018.

5 "Billy Graham: Pastor to Presidents, for More than 50 Years," *Asheville Citizen-Times*, February 21, 2018.

6 Ephrem the Syrian, *Selected Prose Works: Commentary on Genesis, Commentary on Exodus, Homily on Our Lord, Letter to Publius*, ed. K. McVey, trans. Edward Mathews Jr. and Joseph Amar (Washington, D.C.: Catholic University of America Press, 1994), 110–13.

7 Ambrose, *Hexameron, Paradise, and Cain and Abel*, trans. John J. Savage (Washington, D.C.: Catholic University of America Press, 1961), 290.

8 John Chrysostom, *On the Incomprehensible Nature of God*, trans. Paul Harkins (Washington, D.C.: Catholic University of America Press, 1984), 59.

9 Augustine of Hippo, *The City of God: Books VIII–XVI*, trans. Gerald Walsh and Grace Monahan (Washington, D.C.: Catholic University of America Press, 2008), 331.

10 See "The Judgment of Paris," "Hercules and the Golden Apples of the Hesperides," and "Atalanta."

ONE | ANYTHING BUT EXTRAORDINARY

1 Justin's quotation from Dan 7 is an amalgamation of Dan 7 and Rev 13. Neither Masoretic Text (MT) nor Old Greek (OG) nor Theodotion Daniel (Th-Daniel) uses a word rendered as "blasphemous" in Dan 7 to describe the speech of the final horn atop the fourth beast. Revelation 13:5, however, uses βλασφημίας, a word with the primary meaning of "blasphemous," to describe the words of a horn upon the second beast's head. Though it is unclear whether Justin intended to conflate Daniel and Revelation, his work presents an early Christian reading that foreshadows future Christian receptions that consciously read Dan 7 and the fourth beast through the lens of John's Apocalypse.

2 Alexander Roberts and James Donaldson, eds., *Apostolic Fathers, Justin Martyr, Irenaeus*, vol. 1 of *Ante-Nicene Fathers* (New York: Charles Scribner's Sons, 1903); Irénée de Lyon, *Contre les hérésies, Livre IV, Édition critique d'après les versions arménienne et latine 1–2*, éd. Bertrand Hemmerdinger, Louis Doutreleau, and Charles Mercier, Sources chrétiennes 100 (Paris: Cerf, 1965), 928–29.

3 Jerome, *Commentarium in Danielem* 4.8.7: "But now the powerful beast is not one nation, but it is of many tongues and it gathers to itself from many races of men and prepares an army in a line of battle, and all are called Romans, though all are not from one country."

4 Sten Hidal and Knud Jeppesen, "Apocalypse, Persecution and Exegesis: Hippolytus and Theodoret of Cyrrhus on the Book of Daniel," in *In the Last Days: On Jewish and Christian Apocalyptic and Its Period*, ed. Knud Jeppesen, Kirsten Nielsen, and Bent Rosendal (Aarhus, Denmark: Aarhus University Press, 1994), 51.

5 Ephrem the Syrian, *Sancti patris nostri Ephraem Syri Opera omnia*, trans. Peter Ambarach (Rome: Ex typographia Vaticana, Jo. Mariae Henrici Salvioni, 1737–1743), 214.

6 Jerome, *S. Hieronymi Presbyteri Opera, Pars I: Opera Exegetica, 6*; *Commentarii in Prophetas Minores*, ed. M. Adriaen, Corpus Christianorum Series Latina 76 (Turnhout, Belgium: Brepols, 1969): "Quartum quod nunc urbem tenet terrarum, imperium Romanorum est, de quo in statua dicitur."

7 Jerome, *Commentariorum in Danielem* 7.6.

8   Augustine of Hippo, *City of God* 22.23, trans. Henry Bettenson (New York: Penguin, 2004), 1161.

9   Peter Frankopan, *The First Crusade: The Call from the East* (Cambridge, Mass.: Harvard University Press, 2012), 13.

10   Robert Chazan, *God, Humanity, and History: The Hebrew First Crusade Narratives* (Berkeley: University of California Press, 2000), 139.

11   He reads the descriptors of "Atque mirabilis" and "fortis nimis" as applicable to Rome, saying "any of which might fit" the empire. Unless otherwise noted, all citations are from *Andreae De Sancto Victore Opera, I, Expositionem Super Heptateuchum*, ed. C. Lohr and R. Berndt, Corpus Christianorum, Continuatio Medaevalis: Andreae de Sancto Victore Opera 53 (Turnhout, Belgium: Brepols, 1986).

12   Richard Emmerson, "The Representation of Antichrist in Hildegard of Bingen's *Scivias*: Image, Word, Commentary, and Visionary Experience," *Gesta* 41, no. 2 (2002): 97.

13   Steven Runciman, *A History of the Crusades*, vol. 2, *The Kingdom of Jerusalem* (New York: Cambridge University Press, 1995), 143–246.

14   Jennifer Deane, *A History of Medieval Heresy and Inquisition* (Lanham, Md.: Rowman and Littlefield, 2011), 28. She once preached, "You ought to be the corners of the Church's strength, holding her up like the corners that sustain the boundaries of the earth. But you are laid low and do not hold up the Church, retreating instead to the cave of your own desire. And because of the tedium brought on by your riches, avarice, and other vain pursuits, you do not properly teach your subordinates . . . wake up!" See Walter L. Wakefield and Austin P. Evans, *Heresies of the High Middle Ages* (New York: Columbia University Press, 1991), 129.

15   Marjorie Reeves, *Joachim of Fiore and the Prophetic Future* (Cheltenham, UK: Sutton, 1999), 136–65.

16   Reeves, *Joachim of Fiore*, 5. Reeves expands on this, saying that to Joachim, reading the Old Testament in conjunction with the New Testament was logical: "Just as, in the understanding of the individual mind, from meditation on the Letter of the Old and New Testaments there proceeded one Spiritual Intelligence which gathered all truth into one comprehension, so in the history of mankind, from the work of God the Father and God the, there must proceed the work of God the Holy Spirit."

17   Philip Krey, introduction to *Nicholas of Lyra: The Senses of Scripture*, ed. Philip Krey and Lesley Smith (Leiden: Brill, 2000), 1.

18 Philip Krey, "The Law and the Jews in Nicholas of Lyra's Romans Commentary of 1329," in Krey and Smith, *Nicholas of Lyra*, 251–66.

19 Nicholas of Lyra, "Daniel," in *Bibliorum Sacrorum cum Glossa Ordinaria* (Venice, 1603), 4:1579. All translations attributed to Lyra's work with Daniel in the *Glossa* are the author's.

20 Krey, introduction to Krey and Smith, *Nicholas of Lyra*, 5.

21 Nicholas of Lyra, "Daniel," in *Bibliorum Sacrorum cum Glossa Ordinaria*, 4:1577–79.

22 Frans van Liere, "The Literal Sense of the Books of Samuel and Kings: From Andrew of St. Victor to Nicholas of Lyra," in Krey and Smith, *Nicholas of Lyra*, 79.

23 Bernard McGinn, *Visions of the End* (New York: Columbia University Press, 1998), 253–55.

24 Philip Daileader, *Saint Vincent Ferrer, His World and Life* (New York: Palgrave Macmillan, 2016), 2.

25 Vincent Ferrer, "The Report on the Antichrist," in *Historia de la portentosa vida y milagros del Valenciano Apostol de Europa S. Vicente Ferrer, con su misma doctrina reflexionada* (Valencia, Spain: En La Oficina de Joseph Estevan Dolz, 1735), 170: "Tertio: . . . per revelationem factam Danieli Prophetae de decem cornibus quartae bestiae . . . octavo capite."

26 Ferrer, "Report on the Antichrist," in *Historia*, 171. The timeframe in which Ferrer writes overlaps with the break between the cardinals of Avignon's obedience with Pope Benedict XIII in 1398.

27 Winfried Vogel, "The Eschatological Theology of Martin Luther—Part II: Luther's Exposition of Daniel and Revelation," *Andrews University Seminary Studies* 25, no. 2 (1987): 183–85.

28 According to Vogel and other sources, Luther finishes translating Daniel and increases work with the book in 1529. See Vogel, "Eschatological Theology," 184–85.

29 One must also note Luther's staunch and consistent anti-Jewish thread pervasive throughout all of his work. Evangelical interpreters later flip this on its head by being pro-Judaism and pro-Israel but only for the sake of bringing about the second coming. See Donald M. Lewis, *The Origins of Christian Zionism: Lord Shaftesbury and Evangelical Support for a Jewish Homeland* (Cambridge: Cambridge University Press, 2010).

30 Martin Luther. *Luthers Werke: Kritische Gesamtausgabe [Die Deutsche Bibel]*, 12 vols. (Weimar: H. Böhlau, 1883–2009), 11/2:6. Hereafter WA-DB.

31 WA-DB 11/2:6–14.

32 Martin Luther. *Luthers Werke: Kritische Gesamtausgabe [Abteilung Schriften]*, 12 vols. (Weimar: H. Böhlau, 1883–2009), 3:645, 646, no. 3831. Hereafter WA.

33 Martin Luther, *Luther's Works* (*LW*), ed. Jaroslav Pelikan, Helmutt T. Lehman, Christopher Boyd Brown, Benjamin T. G. Mayes, and James Langebartels, American ed., 55 vols. (St. Louis: Concordia; Philadelphia: Fortress, 1955–1986), 10:114; 18:120; 41:198; 35:106–7.

34 WA-DB 11/2:12.

35 WA-DB 11/2:12.

36 Martin Luther, *Luthers Werke: Kritische Gesamtausgabe [Briefwechsel]*, 12 vols. (Weimar: H. Böhlau, 1883–2009), 5:242. Hereafter WA-Br.

37 *LW* 31:393.

38 WA-DB 11/2.124–26.

39 WA-DB 7:414.

40 Joseph Koerner, *The Reformation of the Image* (Chicago: University of Chicago Press, 2004), 116.

41 Koerner, *Reformation of the Image*, 116.

42 Koerner, *Reformation of the Image*, 116–17.

43 Elizabeth Eisenstein, *The Printing Press as an Agent of Change: Communications and Cultural Transformations in Early Modern Europe* (Cambridge: Cambridge University Press, 1979).

44 Barbara Pitkin, "Prophecy and History in Calvin's Lectures on Daniel," in *Die Geschichte der Daniel-Auslegung in Judentum, Christentum und Islam*, ed. Katharina Bracht et al. (Berlin: De Gruyter, 2007), 324.

45 Unless otherwise noted, all translations are the author's. Calvin, *Praelectiones in librum prophetiarum Danielis* (Geneva, 1561). Translations of the lectures appeared in French in 1562 and 1569 and in English in 1570. Two further Latin editions were published in 1571 and 1591. Modern edition in vols. 40–41 of Baum, Cunitz, and Reuss, eds., *Ioannis Calvini opera quae supersunt omnia* (hereafter abbreviated CO and cited by volume number). Quotation from CO XLI 7.7.

46 CO XLI 7.7.

47 Pitkin, "Prophecy and History," 325.

48 CO XLI 7.7.

49 CO XLI 7.7 and CO XLI 7.8.

50 W. Stanford Reid, "The Four Monarchies of Daniel in Reformation Historiography," *Historical Reflections / Réflexions Historiques* 8, no. 1 (1981): 118.

51 CO XLI 7.23.

52 "Vere autem nec unam ob caufam dicitur Romanum regnum formidabile and terrificum: vel ut aln verterut terribile and horrendum." See *Daniel sapientissimus Dei propheta*, 77. References to Heinrich Bullinger's sermons come from *Daniel sapientissimus Dei propheta, qui a vetustis polyhistor, id est musltiscius est dictus, expositus homilus 66 quibus in ecclesia docentibus commonstratui,* Heinrycho Bullingero, Tigurinae ecclesiae ministro (Zurich C. Froschauer, 1565); and *In Apocalypsim Iesu Christi, reuelatam quidem per angelum Domini, uisam uerò uel Exceptam Atque Conscriptam* (London, 1557). See Daniel Timmerman, "The World Always Perishes, the Church Will Last Forever: Church and Eschatology in Bullinger's Sermons on the Book of Daniel (1565)," *Zwingliana* 36 (2009): 85.

53 He discusses this in detail with sermons and commentary, pointing in some cases to the empire's infight as emblematic of its deplorable state. See *Daniel Sapientissimus Dei Propheta* (Zurich: C. Froschouerus, 1576).

54 Per Selnecker, the horns are Syria, Egypt, Asia, Greece, Africa, Spain, France, Italy, Germany, and England.

55 The version consulted for this analysis is a facsimile of the 1566 version of Selnecker's *Der Prophet Daniel, und die Offenbarung Johannis* (Germany: Berwalt, 1567).

56 John Calvin, *Commentaries on the Book of the Prophet Daniel,* in *Calvin's Commentaries,* 45 vols. (Edinburgh, 1844–1856); reprinted in 22 vols. (Grand Rapids: Baker, 1981). Hereafter CC. CC 13, Lec. 50.

57 James Brashler, "From Erasmus to Calvin: Exploring the Roots of Reformed Hermeneutics," *Interpretation* 63, no. 2 (2009): 166.

58 Brashler, "From Erasmus to Calvin," 166.

59 Oecolampadius, *Commentariorum in Danielem Prophetam* 91.

60 W. Brian Shelton, *Martyrdom from Exegesis in Hippolytus: An Early Church Presbyter's Commentary on Daniel* (Eugene, Ore.: Wipf and Stock, 2008), 71.

TWO | THE ROOTS OF GRAHAM'S APOCALYPTIC NATIONALISM

1 John Edwards, *A Compleat History or Survey of All the Dispensations* (London, 1699), v.

2 Charles C. Ryrie, *Dispensationalism* (Chicago: Moody, 1995), 52.

3 Ryrie, *Dispensationalism*, 53.

4 Ryrie, *Dispensationalism*, 54–55.

5 Mark Noll, *A History of Christianity in the United States and Canada* (Grand Rapids: Eerdmans, 1992), 377–78.

6 Cyrus I. Scofield, introduction to *The Scofield Reference Bible*, ed. and annotated by Cyrus I. Scofield (New York: Oxford University Press, 1917).

7 Cyrus I. Scofield, *Rightly Dividing the Word of Truth* (1888; citations refer to the PDF version available at http://biblecentre.org/content.php?mode=7&item=777, 11–13).

8 George Truett, "Baptists and Religious Liberty" (sermon, Washington, D.C., 1920), http://www.reformedreader.org/baptistsandreligiousliberty.htm.

9 It is worth noting the Ku Klux Klan took resistance to Italian-Catholic immigration as a chance for growth, and grow it did, as the organization experienced a period of expansion during the post-WWI years that spring-boarded it to more hate-filled destructive power in the 1940s, 1950s, and 1960s.

10 Truett, "Baptists and Religious Liberty."

11 Truett, "Baptists and Religious Liberty."

12 Truett, "Baptists and Religious Liberty."

13 Garth Rosell, *The Surprising Work of God: Harold John Ockenga, Billy Graham, and the Rebirth of Evangelicalism* (Grand Rapids: Baker, 2008).

14 Harold Ockenga, "The Ethiopian Situation, or The Meaning of the Present World Crisis" (sermon, 1935).

15 Harold Ockenga, "God Save America" (sermon, September 1939).

16 John R. Rice, "Is Mussolini the Anti-Christ?" *Sword of the Lord* 1, no. 9 (1935): 1.

17 William Bell Riley, "The Kingdom of God—Its Location," *The Northwestern Pilot*, July 1954, 11–12.

18 Riley, "Kingdom of God," 15.

19 William Bell Riley, "Coming Armageddon" (sermon, First Baptist Church Minneapolis, 1940), 3, https://cdm16120.contentdm.oclc.org/digital/collection/riley/id/3694/rec/4.

20 Riley, "Coming Armageddon," 4–5.

21 Riley, "Coming Armageddon," 8.

22 Darren Dochuk addresses the impact of these social and economic movements and addresses their roots, calling them a "populist legacy." Dochuk speaks directly to the spirit of limited "egalitarianism"

during the growth and development of the American South. He argues, "White plain folk living on the east side of the Mississippi could not extend the ideals of egalitarianism too far for fear of jeopardizing their racial privileges." See Dochuk, *From Bible Belt to Sun Belt* (New York: Norton, 2012), 9–10.

23 W. A. Criswell, "Knowing the Time" (sermon, First Baptist Church of Dallas, January 16, 1955), https://wacriswell.com/sermons/1955/knowing-the-time/.

24 Joe Early Jr., "W. A. Criswell: The Wall of Separation of Church and State and Politics," *Baptist History and Heritage* 43, no. 3 (2008): 83 and 87.

25 W. A. Criswell, "The Purpose of Prophecy" (sermon, Dallas, January 9, 1972), https://wacriswell.com/sermons/1958/purpose-of-prophecy/.

26 W. A. Criswell, "The Way Back to God" (sermon, December 31, 1944), https://wacriswell.com/sermons/1944/the-way-back-to-god/.

27 W. A. Criswell, "George Truett and Religious Liberty" (sermon, July 3, 1960), https://wacriswell.com/sermons/1960/george-truett-and-religious-liberty/.

28 W. A. Criswell, "Dr. Truett and God's Call to America" (sermon, July 4, 1965), https://wacriswell.com/sermons/1965/dr-truett-and-god-s-call-to-america-2/.

29 W. A. Criswell, "Daniel and Revelation," in *Expository Sermons on the Book of Daniel* (Grand Rapids: Zondervan, 1976), 1:113.

30 Criswell, "Daniel and Revelation," in *Expository Sermons*, 1:113.

31 Criswell, "Daniel and Revelation," in *Expository Sermons*, 1:113.

32 Criswell, "Daniel and Revelation," in *Expository Sermons*, 1:123.

33 W. A. Criswell, "The Beast Nations" (sermon, Dallas, January 16, 1972), https://wacriswell.com/sermons/1972/the-beast-nations/.

34 Criswell, "The Beast Nations"

35 W. A. Criswell, "The Changes I Have Seen in My Life" (sermon, First Baptist Church, Swannanoa, N.C., April 18, 1993), https://wacriswell.com/sermons/1993/the-changes-i-have-seen-in-my-life/.

36 William Martin, *A Prophet with Honor: The Billy Graham Story* (Grand Rapids: Zondervan, 2018).

THREE | BILLY GRAHAM'S APOCALYPTIC WORLDVIEW

1 Jonathan Merritt, "Billy Graham, the Last Nonpartisan Evangelical?" *New York Times*, February 21, 2018.

2   Billy Graham, "The Love of God (Part 1)" (sermon, Baltimore, 2006), https://billygraham.org/audio/the-love-of-god-part-1/.

3   Billy Graham, "The Second Coming of Christ" (sermon, Los Angeles, 1949), https://billygraham.org/audio/the-second-coming-of-christ/; and "The Rise of the AntiChrist" (sermon, *Hour of Decision*, 1972), https://billygraham.org/audio/the-rise-of-the-antichrist/.

4   Billy Graham, "Why God Allows Communism to Flourish" (sermon, Los Angeles, 1949), https://billygraham.org/audio/why-god-allows -communism-to-flourish/.

5   Graham, "Why God Allows Communism."

6   Graham, "Why God Allows Communism."

7   Graham, "Why God Allows Communism."

8   Graham, "Why God Allows Communism."

9   Billy Graham, "Final Judgment" (sermon, Los Angeles, 1949), https://billygraham.org/audio/final-judgment/.

10 Graham, "Final Judgment."

11 Graham, "Final Judgment."

12 Graham, "Final Judgment."

13 Graham, "Final Judgment."

14 Graham, "Final Judgment."

15 Graham, "Second Coming."

16 Graham, "Second Coming."

17 Graham, "Second Coming." This statement is consistent with Graham's later biographic works, as his mother's conversion via Revelation shaped Graham's Christian worldview. See chapter 2, "The 180-Degree Turn," in Graham's autobiography, *Just as I Am* (San Francisco: HarperCollins, 1997), for further detail about Graham's mother, her theological leanings, and her tenacity that led to Graham's eventual conversion.

18 Graham, "Second Coming."

19 Graham, "Second Coming."

20 Graham, "Second Coming."

21 Graham, "Second Coming."

22 Billy Graham, "Request for Prayer for Washington" (sermon, Greensboro, N.C., 1951), https://billygraham.org/audio/request-for-prayer -for-washington/.

23 Billy Graham, "America's Need for Spiritual Awakening" (sermon, Pittsburgh, 1952), https://billygraham.org/audio/americas-need-for -spiritual-awakening/.

24 Graham, "America's Need."

25 Dwight D. Eisenhower, "The Chance for Peace" (speech, Washington, D.C., April 16, 1953).

26 Eisenhower, "Chance for Peace."

27 Billy Graham, "Communism and Christianity" (sermon, Little Rock, Ark., 1953), https://billygraham.org/audio/communism-and-christianity/.

28 Billy Graham, "Warnings to America" (sermon, SS *United States*, 1954), https://billygraham.org/audio/warnings-to-america/.

29 Graham, "Warnings."

30 Graham, "Warnings."

31 Graham, "Warnings."

32 Billy Graham, "Ways America May Continue to Prosper" (sermon, New Orleans, 1954), https://billygraham.org/audio/ways-america-may-continue-to-prosper/.

33 Graham, "Ways America."

34 Graham, "Ways America."

35 Billy Graham, "Christ Is Coming" (sermon, *Hour of Decision*, 1955), https://billygraham.org/audio/christ-is-coming/.

36 Billy Graham, "Our Nation Must Repent" (sermon, *Hour of Decision*, 1957), https://billygraham.org/audio/our-nation-must-repent/.

37 Graham, "Our Nation."

38 Billy Graham, "The Handwriting on the Wall" (sermon, San Francisco, 1958), https://billygraham.org/audio/the-handwriting-on-the-wall/.

39 Graham, "Handwriting."

40 Billy Graham, "The End of the World" (Montreat, N.C., 1958), https://billygraham.org/audio/the-end-of-the-world/.

41 Billy Graham, "The Supreme Court Ruling on Prayer" (sermon, Minneapolis, 1962), https://billygraham.org/audio/the-supreme-court-ruling-on-prayer/. It is worth noting that Graham's "quotation" restates the sentiment more than the quote itself, which is "that the ruling could put the United States schools on the same basis as Russian schools." See Robert Alley, *School Prayer: The Court, The Congress, and the First Amendment* (Amherst, N.Y.: Prometheus Books, 1994), 109.

42 Billy Graham, "Learning from National Tragedy: A Message from Billy Graham" (sermon, Minneapolis, 1963), https://billygraham.org/audio/how-could-it-happen-in-america/.

43 Billy Graham, *World Aflame* (New York: Doubleday, 1965), 8.

44 Graham, *World Aflame*, 174.

45 Graham, *World Aflame*, 45.

46 Graham, *World Aflame*, 169 (emphasis added).

47 Billy Graham, "Preparation for Armageddon" (sermon, Minneapolis, 1967), https://billygraham.org/audio/preparation-for-armageddon/.

48 Billy Graham, "America Is in Trouble" (sermon, Minneapolis, 1967), https://billygraham.org/audio/america-is-in-trouble/.

49 Graham, "America Is in Trouble."

50 Graham, "America Is in Trouble."

51 Billy Graham, "Shadows of the Great Antichrist" (sermon, Minneapolis, 1967), https://billygraham.org/audio/shadows-of-the-great-antichrist/.

52 Graham, "Shadows."

53 Graham, "Shadows."

54 Graham, "Shadows."

55 Billy Graham, "Can America Survive?" (sermon, Minneapolis, 1968), https://billygraham.org/audio/can-american-survive/.

56 Billy Graham, "America's Greatest Need" (sermon, Minneapolis, 1969).

57 Graham, "America's Greatest."

58 Billy Graham, "The Coming Kingdom" (sermon, Minneapolis, 1970), https://billygraham.org/audio/the-coming-kingdom/.

59 Graham, "Coming Kingdom."

60 Billy Graham, "America, Is the Handwriting on the Wall?" (sermon, St. Louis, 1973), https://billygraham.org/audio-cat/sermons/?s=is+the+handwriting+on+the+wall.

61 Graham, "America, Is the Handwriting."

62 Graham, "America, Is the Handwriting."

63 Billy Graham, "The Coming Storm" (sermon, Tempe, Ariz., 1974), https://billygraham.org/audio/the-coming-storm/.

64 Billy Graham, *Approaching Hoofbeats: The Four Horsemen of the Apocalypse* (Waco, Tex.: Word, 1983), 27.

65 Graham, *Approaching Hoofbeats*, 74 and 76.

66 Graham, *Approaching Hoofbeats*, 74.

67 Graham, *Approaching Hoofbeats*, 76.

68 Billy Graham, "When Will the End of the World Come?" (sermon, Bristol, England, 1984), https://billygraham.org/audio/when-will-the-end-of-the-world-come-2/.

69 Graham, "When."

70 Graham, "When."

71 Graham, "When."

72 Billy Graham, "Dare to Be a Daniel" (sermon, Columbia, S.C., 1987), https://billygraham.org/audio/dare-to-be-a-daniel/.

73 Billy Graham, *Storm Warning* (Dallas: Word, 1992), 7.

74 Graham, *Storm Warning* (1992), 8.

75 Graham, *Storm Warning* (1992), 9.

76 Laurie Goodstein, "Billy Graham, 99, Dies; Pastor Filled Stadiums and Counseled Presidents," *New York Times*, February 21, 2018.

77 Billy Graham, *Storm Warning* (Nashville: Thomas Nelson, 2011), 86. Matthew Avery Sutton astutely points to a likely jab at then-president Obama when Graham (p. 186) writes, "We are called to distinguish ourselves as Christ-followers, not community organizers." See Sutton, *American Apocalypse: A History of Modern Evangelicalism* (Cambridge, Mass.: Belknap Press of Harvard University Press, 2014), 373.

78 Graham, *Storm Warning* (2011), 86.

FOUR | PREACHER, PASTOR, AND PRESIDENT

1 Kevin Kruse, *One Nation under God: How Corporate America Invented Christian America* (New York: Basic Books, 2015), xii.

2 Patrick Henry, "'And I Don't Care What It Is': The Tradition-History of a Civil Religion Proof-Text," *Journal of the American Academy of Religion* 49, no. 1 (1981): 41.

3 For a detailed dive into the link between American evangelicals and modern Israeli Jews, see chapter 2, "Global War and Christian Nationalism," in Sutton's *American Apocalypse*.

4 Tobin Grant, "Why 1940s America Wasn't as Religious as You Think—the Rise and Fall of American Religion," *Religion News Service*, December 11, 2014, https://religionnews.com/2014/12/11/1940s-america-wasnt-religious-think-rise-fall-american-religion/.

5 Frank Newport, "Five Key Findings on Religion in the U.S.," *Gallup*, December 23, 2016, https://news.gallup.com/poll/200186/five-key-findings-religion.aspx.

6 Dwight D. Eisenhower, *Papers of Dwight David Eisenhower* (Baltimore: Johns Hopkins University Press, 1970), 1:366.

7 Dwight D. Eisenhower, *Crusade in Europe* (Garden City, N.Y.: Doubleday, 1948), 106.

8 Eisenhower, *Papers*, 18:190.

9   Jerry Bergman, "Steeped in Religion: President Eisenhower and the Influence of the Jehovah's Witnesses," *Kansas History* 21, no. 3 (1998): 149.

10 Bergman, "Steeped in Religion," 152.

11 N. H. Knorr, "Religion Void of Principle," *Awake!*, October 22, 1946, 7.

12 Knorr, "Religion Void of Principle," 7.

13 Eisenhower, *Crusade in Europe*, 106.

14 Nina Golgowski, "Evangelical Christian Billy Graham Stops Calling Mormonism a 'Cult' to Help Romney into the White House," *Daily Mail.com*, October 18, 2012, https://www.dailymail.co.uk/news/article-2219364/Evangelistic-Association-Reverend-Billy-Graham-stops-calling-Mormonism-cult-meeting-Romney.html.

15 James Farrell, "Thomas Merton and the Religion of the Bomb," *Religion and American Culture: A Journal of Interpretation* 5, no. 1 (1995): 79–80

16 Ben Bagdikian, *The Media Monopoly* (Boston: Beacon, 2000), 39.

17 Nancy Gibbs and Michael Duffy, *The Preacher and the Presidents* (New York: Hachette, 2007), 24.

18 Billy Graham, "National Repentance" (sermon, Washington, D.C., 1952), https://billygraham.org/audio/national-repentance/.

19 Harry S. Truman, "Inaugural Address," Washington, D.C., January 20, 1949, https://avalon.law.yale.edu/20th_century/truman.asp.

20 Gibbs and Duffy, *Preacher and the Presidents*, 25.

21 Martin Marty, *Modern American Religion*, vol. 3, *Under God, Indivisible, 1941–1960* (Chicago: University of Chicago Press, 1996), 305.

22 Gibbs and Duffy, *Preacher and the Presidents*, 32.

23 Ralph Lord Roy, *Apostles of Discord* (Boston: Beacon, 1953), 20.

24 Gibbs and Duffy (*Preacher and the Presidents*) repeatedly deny any notion of Graham having direct influence on Eisenhower beyond the president's spiritual perspectives, but Graham's praise and guidance of Eisenhower created a bond, one whose ripple effects remained, as evidenced through Graham's continued relationships with powerful political leaders.

25 Billy Graham, "Mr. President" (sermon, St. Louis, 1953), https://billygraham.org/audio/mr-president/.

26 Graham, *Storm Warning*, 232.

27 Graham, *Storm Warning*, 232. Graham cites the following: "Every gun that is made, every warship launched, every rocket fired signifies—in the final sense—a theft from those who hunger and

are not fed, those who are cold and are not clothed. This world in arms is not spending money alone. It is spending the sweat of its laborers, the genius of its scientists, the hopes of its children. . . . This is not a way of life at all, in any true sense. Under the cloud of war, it is humanity hanging on a cross of iron."

28 *New York Times*, June 15, 1954.

29 *New York Times*, June 15, 1954.

30 Charles Oakman, "Abraham Lincoln: Extension of Remarks of Hon. Charles G. Oakman," *Congressional Record*, vol. 100, session 2 (February 12, 1954), 1697.

31 Ferguson includes a manuscript of the entire sermon in his follow-up, which is recorded in an appendix for the Proceedings of Congress from March 3, 1954, through April 2, 1954, on page A1794.

32 Billy Graham, "Prepare to Meet Thy God" (sermon, Washington, D.C., 1952), https://billygraham.org/audio/prepare-to-meet-thy-god/.

33 Graham, "National Repentance."

34 George Docherty, *I've Seen the Day* (Grand Rapids: Eerdmans, 1984), 172.

35 Docherty, *I've Seen the Day*, 158.

36 Docherty, *I've Seen the Day*, 170.

37 Docherty, *I've Seen the Day*, 160.

38 Alan Reitman, memorandum to the Washington office, May 24, 1954, Box 1, ACLU.

39 "Constitutional Amendments and Religious Liberty," *Christian Century*, May 26, 1954.

40 Gibbs and Duffy, *Preacher and the Presidents*, 82.

41 Marshall Frady, *Billy Graham: A Parable of American Righteousness* (New York: Simon and Schuster, 2006), 445.

42 Gibbs and Duffy, *Preacher and the Presidents*, 101–2.

FIVE | EVANGELICAL NATIONALISM AFTER EISENHOWER

1 *New York Times*, June 27, 1962.

2 Kruse, *One Nation*, 186.

3 Kruse, *One Nation*, 186.

4 Billy Graham, "Reverend Billy Graham's Reaction following the Assassination of President John F. Kennedy" (speech, Dallas, November 1963), https://www.youtube.com/watch?v=PsjlnHHZYjk.

5 Lyndon Baines Johnson, "President Johnson's Special Message to Congress: The American Promise," March 15, 1965, video and transcript,

LBJ Presidential Library, http://www.lbjlibrary.org/lyndon-baines
-johnson/speeches-films/president-johnsons-special-message-to
-the-congress-the-american-promise/.

6   "Here are Twenty Reasons WHY you should, if qualified, join, aid
and support the White Knights of the KU KLUX KLAN of Mississippi," http://law2.umkc.edu/faculty/projects/ftrials/price&bowers/
Klan.html.

7   Richard Nixon, *The Memoirs of Richard Nixon* (New York: Grosset
and Dunlap, 1978).

8   Sarah Pulliam Bailey, "Q & A: Billy Graham on Aging, Regrets, and
Evangelicals," *Christianity Today*, January 21, 2011, https://www
.christianitytoday.com/ct/2011/januaryweb-only/qabillygraham
.html.

9   Gerald Ford, "President Gerald R. Ford's Remarks on Signing
a Proclamation Granting Pardon to Richard Nixon," Washington, D.C., September 1974, https://www.fordlibrarymuseum.gov/
library/speeches/740060.asp.

10 Philip Shabecoff, "Presidency Is Found Weaker under Ford," *New
York Times*, March 28, 1976.

11 Gerald Ford, "1976 State of the Union," Washington, D.C.

12 Gibbs and Duffy, *Preacher and the Presidents*, 272. Carter addressed
his relationship with Graham directly: "[Rosalynn and I] had
observed that my predecessors had invited Billy Graham and
other famous preachers to conduct well-publicized worship services in the White House. We respected their right to do so, but
we felt that for us to do the same would violate our concept of
church and state being kept separate." Carter changed his position and invited many religious leaders, including Graham, once
he saw the growing political power of the Moral Majority. Randall Balmer, *Redeemer: The Life of Jimmy Carter* (New York: Basic
Books, 2014), 128–29.

13 Jimmy Carter, "Address to the Nation on Energy and National
Goals: 'Crisis of Confidence,'" July 15, 1979, https://www.pbs.org/
wgbh/americanexperience/features/carter-crisis/.

14 Ronald Reagan, "A Time for Choosing," in *The U.S. Constitution:
A Reader*, ed. Hillsdale College Politics Faculty (Hillsdale, Mich.:
Hillsdale College Press, 2012), 783.

15 James Mills, "The Serious Implications of a 1971 Conversation with
Ronald Reagan," *San Diego Magazine*, August 1985.

16 Ronald Reagan, "1980 Republican National Convention Acceptance Speech," July 17, 1980, https://millercenter.org/the-presidency/presidential-speeches/july-17-1980-republican-national-convention.

17 Ronald Reagan, "Inaugural Address, January 20, 1981," in *Public Papers of the Presidents: Ronald Reagan 1981* (Washington, D.C.: United States Government Printing Office, 1982).

18 Ronald Reagan, *The Reagan Diaries*, ed. Douglas Brinkley (New York: Harper Collins, 2007), 19.

19 Reagan, *Diaries*, 24.

20 Reagan, *Diaries*, 150.

21 Ronald Reagan, "State of the Union Address," January 26, 1982, https://millercenter.org/the-presidency/presidential-speeches/january-26-1982-state-union-address.

22 Ronald Reagan, "Evil Empire," March 8, 1983, https://millercenter.org/the-presidency/presidential-speeches/march-8-1983-evil-empire-speech.

23 Ronald Reagan, "State of the Union Address," January 25, 1983, https://millercenter.org/the-presidency/presidential-speeches/january-25-1983-state-union-address.

24 *Engel v. Vitale*, 370 U.S. 421 (1962).

25 Ronald Reagan, "Republican National Convention Acceptance Speech," August 23, 1984, https://millercenter.org/the-presidency/presidential-speeches/august-23-1984-republican-national-convention.

26 Ronald Reagan, "Remarks at an Ecumenical Prayer Breakfast in Dallas, Texas" (speech, Dallas, August 23, 1984), https://www.reaganfoundation.org/media/128825/dallas.pdf.

27 Reagan, "Remarks at an Ecumenical Prayer Breakfast."

28 Capitalization of "Author" is Reagan's choice.

29 Ronald Reagan, "Second Inaugural Address," January 21, 1985, https://millercenter.org/the-presidency/presidential-speeches/january-21-1985-second-inaugural-address.

30 Ronald Reagan, "State of the Union," February 6, 1985, https://millercenter.org/the-presidency/presidential-speeches/february-6-1985-state-union-address.

31 Ronald Reagan, "State of the Union," February 4, 1986, https://millercenter.org/the-presidency/presidential-speeches/february-4-1986-state-union-address.

32 Ronald Reagan, "Farewell Address at the Republican National Convention," August 15, 1988, https://millercenter.org/the-presidency/presidential-speeches/august-15-1988-farewell-address-republican-national-convention.

33 Reprint of American Atheist booklet, taken from the website for the National Secular Society: "George Bush on Atheists as Citizens or Patriots," February 6, 2004, https://www.secularism.org.uk/33034.html. Bush confirmes this sentiment toward atheists in an interview with Don Imus in September 2004. "'We Are Better Off Today,' Says George H. W. Bush," *NBC News*, September 1, 2004, http://www.nbcnews.com/id/5889684/ns/msnbc-imus_on_msnbc/t/we-are-better-today-says-george-h-w-bush/#.XpY5tchKhz1.

34 George H. W. Bush, "State of the Union Address," January 31, 1990, https://millercenter.org/the-presidency/presidential-speeches/january-31-1990-state-union-address.

35 For a more detailed look at Clinton's religious background, see "Chapter 10: Bill Clinton—Sin, Atonement, and Repairing the Breach," in Gary Scott Smith, *Religion in the Oval Office* (New York: Oxford University Press, 2015).

36 Marc Lacey, "Clinton Ranks In the Middle, But Falls Last On Morality," *New York Times*, February 21, 2000, https://www.nytimes.com/2000/02/21/us/clinton-ranks-in-the-middle-but-falls-last-on-morality.html.

37 Bill Clinton, "State of the Union Address," January 27, 2000, https://millercenter.org/the-presidency/presidential-speeches/january-27-2000-state-union-address. Emphasis mine.

38 Deborah Orin, "Bush: One Nation, under God," *New York Post*, July 5, 2002, https://nypost.com/2002/07/05/bush-one-nation-under-god/.

39 *Elk Grove Unified School District v. Newdow* (2004).

40 "S.2690 – A Bill to Reaffirm the Reference to One Nation under God in the Pledge of Allegiance," Congress.gov, https://www.congress.gov/bill/107th-congress/senate-bill/2690/text.

41 Barack Obama, "Remarks on the Death of Osama bin Laden," May 1, 2011, video and transcript, Miller Center, University of Virginia, https://millercenter.org/the-presidency/presidential-speeches/may-1-2011-remarks-death-osama-bin-laden.

42 Barack Obama, "Address to Congress on the American Jobs Act," September 8, 2011, video and transcript, Miller Center, University

of Virginia, https://millercenter.org/the-presidency/presidential-speeches/september-8-2011-address-congress-american-jobs-act.

43 Ashley Parker, "In Romney's Hands, Pledge of Allegiance Is Framework for Criticism," *New York Times*, September 8, 2012, https://www.nytimes.com/2012/09/09/us/politics/romney-uses-pledge-of-allegiance-to-criticize-obama.html?auth=linked-google.

44 Abby Ohlheiser, "Why President Obama Didn't Say 'under God' while Reading the Gettysburg Address," *Yahoo! News*, November 19, 2013, https://news.yahoo.com/why-president-obama-didnt-under-god-while-reading-191035734.html.

45 Sarah McCammon, "What Does Trump's Promise of a Nation 'under One God' Really Mean?" *NPR*, September 18, 2016, https://www.npr.org/2016/09/18/494367803/what-does-trumps-promise-of-a-nation-under-one-god-really-mean.

46 "Donald Trump Campaign Rally in Des Moines, Iowa," September 13, 2016, video and transcript, C-SPAN, https://www.c-span.org/video/?415184-1%2Fdonald-trump-campaigns-des-moines-iowa; "Donald Trump Union League of Philadelphia Full Speech," YouTube video, posted September 7, 2016, https://www.youtube.com/watch?v=6BpuNbXDpoQ; https://www.c-span.org/video/?415085-1/donald-trump-campaigns-ashville-north-carolina. It is also worth noting that Democrat Barack Obama won Iowa, Pennsylvania, and North Carolina in 2008, and Iowa and Pennsylvania in 2012.

47 Brian Klaas, "A Short History of President Trump's Anti-Muslim Bigotry," *Washington Post*, March 15, 2019, https://www.washingtonpost.com/opinions/2019/03/15/short-history-president-trumps-anti-muslim-bigotry/. Jenna Johnson and Abigail Hauslohner, "'I Think Islam Hates Us': A Timeline of Trump's Comments about Islam and Muslims," *Washington Post*, March 20, 2017, https://www.washingtonpost.com/news/post-politics/wp/2017/05/20/i-think-islam-hates-us-a-timeline-of-trumps-comments-about-islam-and-muslims/.

48 Donald J. Trump, "We Believe that Every American Should Stand for the National Anthem, and We Proudly Pledge Allegiance to One NATION UNDER GOD!" Twitter, December 9, 2017, https://twitter.com/realdonaldtrump/status/939375570919612416?lang=en.

49 William Cummings, "Trump Claims Americans Say 'under God' and 'Merry Christmas' More since He Won," *USA Today*, May 3, 2018, https://www.usatoday.com/story/news/politics/onpolitics/2018/05/03/trump-americans-saying-under-god-more/578069002/.

50 "Trump to Anthem Protesters: 'Get That Son of a B—— Off the Field,'" *NBC Sports*, September 22, 2017. https://www.nbcsports.com/bayarea/49ers/trump-anthem-protesters-get-son-b-field.

51 Donald J. Trump, "Speech at the Veterans of Foreign Wars National Convention," July 24, 2018, video and transcript, Miller Center, University of Virginia, https://millercenter.org/the-presidency/presidential-speeches/july-24-2018-speech-veterans-foreign-wars-national-convention.

52 "One GLORIOUS Nation under God," YouTube video, posted January 3, 2020, https://www.youtube.com/watch?v=44AiTIFRgfw.

53 Donald J. Trump, "Remarks by President Trump at the National Day of Prayer," May 3, 2018, WhiteHouse.gov, https://trumpwhitehouse.archives.gov/briefings-statements/remarks-president-trump-national-day-prayer/.

54 Donald J. Trump, "State of the Union Address," February 5, 2019, video and transcript, Miller Center, University of Virginia, https://millercenter.org/the-presidency/presidential-speeches/february-5-2019-state-union-address.

55 "President Donald J. Trump Stands Up for Religious Freedom in the United States," May 3, 2018, WhiteHouse.gov, https://trumpwhitehouse.archives.gov/briefings-statements/president-donald-j-trump-stands-religious-freedom-united-states/.

CONCLUSION

1 Jack Jenkins, "Ahead of Trump Bible Photo Op, Police Forcibly Expel Priest from St. John's Church near White House," *Religion News Service*, June 3, 2020, https://religionnews.com/2020/06/02/ahead-of-trump-bible-photo-op-police-forcibly-expel-priest-from-st-johns-church-near-white-house/.

2 It should also be noted that mere hours after the completion of the 2020 Democratic National Convention, Donald Trump took to Twitter and claimed that the Democrats "took the word GOD out of the Pledge of Allegiance" during its recitations that week. He urged evangelicals to heed his warning: "At first I thought they made a mistake, but it wasn't. It was done on purpose. Remember Evangelical Christians, and ALL, this is where they are coming from—it's done. Vote Nov[ember] 3!" The president was incorrect and passed along this false claim. Martin Pengelly, "Trump Spreads False Claim Democrats Dropped God from Pledge of Allegiance,"

Guardian, August 22, 2020, https://www.theguardian.com/us-news/2020/aug/22/donald-trump-democrats-god-pledge.

3   Paul LeBlanc, "Bishop at DC Church Outraged by Trump Visit: 'I Just Can't Believe What My Eyes Have Seen,'" *CNN*, June 2, 2020, https://www.cnn.com/2020/06/01/politics/cnntv-bishop-trump-photo-op/index.html.

4   It is worth noting that Graham here is incorrect: the church had little to no visible vandalism and had not been set on fire. Church leaders ordered their windows boarded up as a precautionary measure.

5   McKay Coppins, "The Christians Who Loved Trump's Stunt," *Atlantic*, June 3, 2020, https://www.theatlantic.com/politics/archive/2020/06/trumps-biblical-spectacle-outside-st-johns-church/612529/.

6   Peter Wehner, "Are Trump's Critics Demonically Possessed?" *Atlantic*, November 25, 2019, https://www.theatlantic.com/ideas/archive/2019/11/to-trumps-evangelicals-everyone-else-is-a-sinner/602569/.

7   Wehner, "Trump's Critics."

8   Wehner, "Trump's Critics."

9   Wehner, "Trump's Critics."

10   Bradley Blackburn, "The Rev. Franklin Graham Says President Obama Was 'Born a Muslim,'" *ABC News*, August 20, 2010, https://abcnews.go.com/WN/franklin-graham-president-obama-born-muslim-pew-poll/story?id=11446462.

11   A group called "Vote Common Good," run by evangelical pastor Doug Pagitt, began working in 2020 to move evangelical voters away from voting for Donald Trump. In September 2020, they shared an ad in which Billy Graham rails against corrupted leadership and false messiahs, juxtaposed with images and sound bites from Trump's presidency as evidence and support.

12   Statistic based on a basic search using the engine from www.google.com on August 23, 2019, 2:27 p.m. The search terms were limited to, as stated above, "Under God in Daniel" and "Under God in Revelation."

BIBLIOGRAPHY

Alley, Robert. *School Prayer: The Court, The Congress, and the First Amendment.* Amherst, N.Y.: Prometheus Books, 1994.

Ambrose. *Hexameron, Paradise, and Cain and Abel.* Translated by John J. Savage. Washington, D.C.: Catholic University of America Press, 1961.

Andrew of St. Victor. *Andreae De Sancto Victore Opera, I, Expositionem Super Heptateuchum.* Vol. 53. Corpus Christianorum. Continuatio Mediaevalis. Edited by Lohr, C., and R. Berndt. Turnhout, Belgium: Typographi Brepols Editores Pontificii, 1986.

Auberlen, Karl August. *Der Prophet Daniel Und Die Offenbarung Johannis.* 2nd ed. Basel: Bahnmaier (Detloff), 1857.

Augustine of Hippo. *City of God.* Translated by Henry Bettenson. New York: Penguin, 2004.

———. *The City of God: Books VIII–XVI.* Translated by Gerald Walsh and Grace Monahan. Washington, D.C.: Catholic University of America Press, 2008.

Bagdikian, Ben. *The Media Monopoly.* Boston: Beacon, 2000.

Bailey, Sarah Pulliam. "Q & A: Billy Graham on Aging, Regrets, and Evangelicals." *Christianity Today,* January 21, 2011. https://www.christianitytoday.com/ct/2011/januaryweb-only/qabillygraham.html.

Balmer, Randall. *Redeemer: The Life of Jimmy Carter.* New York: Basic Books, 2014.

Bergman, Jerry. "Steeped in Religion: President Eisenhower and the Influence of the Jehovah's Witnesses." *Kansas History* 21, no. 3 (1998): 148–67.

"Billy Graham: Pastor to Presidents, for More than 50 Years." *Asheville Citizen-Times.* February 21, 2018.

Blackburn, Bradley. "The Rev. Franklin Graham Says President Obama Was 'Born a Muslim.'" *ABC News*, August 20, 2010. https://abcnews .go.com/WN/franklin-graham-president-obama-born-muslim-pew -poll/story?id=11446462.

Brashler, James. "From Erasmus to Calvin: Exploring the Roots of Reformed Hermeneutics." *Interpretation* 63, no. 2 (2009): 154–66.

Bullinger, Heinrich. *Daniel sapientissimus Dei propheta, qui a vetustis polyhistor, id est musltiscius est dictus, expositus homilus 66 quibus in ecclesia docentibus commonstratui.* Heinrycho Bullingero, Tigurinae ecclesiae ministro. Zurich C. Froschauer, 1565.

———. *In Apocalysim Iesu Christi, reuelatam quidem per angelum Domini, uisam uerò uel Exceptam Atque Conscriptam.* London, 1557.

Bush, George H. W. "State of the Union Address." January 31, 1990. https://millercenter.org/the-presidency/presidential-speeches/ january-31-1990-state-union-address.

Calvin, John. *Commentaries on the Book of the Prophet Daniel.* In *Calvin's Commentaries.* 45 vols. Edinburgh, 1844–1856. Reprinted in 22 vols., Grand Rapids: Baker, 1981.

———. *Praelectiones in librum prophetiarum Danielis.* Geneva, 1561.

Carter, Jimmy. "Address to the Nation on Energy and National Goals: 'Crisis of Confidence.'" July 15, 1979. https://www.pbs.org/wgbh/ americanexperience/features/carter-crisis/.

Chazan, Robert. *God, Humanity, and History: The Hebrew First Crusade Narratives.* Berkeley: University of California Press, 2000.

Chrysostom, John. *On the Incomprehensible Nature of God.* Translated by Paul Harkins. Washington, D.C.: Catholic University of America Press, 1984.

Clinton, Bill. "State of the Union Address." January 27, 2000. https:// millercenter.org/the-presidency/presidential-speeches/january-27 -2000-state-union-address.

"Constitutional Amendments and Religious Liberty." *Christian Century.* May 26, 1954.

Coppins, McKay. "The Christians Who Loved Trump's Stunt." *Atlantic,* June 3, 2020. https://www.theatlantic.com/politics/archive/2020/06/ trumps-biblical-spectacle-outside-st-johns-church/612529/.

Criswell, W. A. "The Beast Nations." Sermon, Dallas, January 16, 1972. https://wacriswell.com/sermons/1972/the-beast-nations/.

———. "The Changes I Have Seen in My Life." Sermon, First Baptist Church, Swannanoa, N.C., April 18, 1993. https://wacriswell.com/sermons/1993/the-changes-i-have-seen-in-my-life/.

———. "Dr. Truett and God's Call to America." Sermon, First Baptist Church, Dallas, TX. July 4, 1965. https://wacriswell.com/sermons/1965/dr-truett-and-god-s-call-to-america-2/.

———. *Expository Sermons on the Book of Daniel.* Grand Rapids: Zondervan, 1976.

———. "George Truett and Religious Liberty." Sermon, First Baptist Church, Dallas, TX. July 3, 1960. https://wacriswell.com/sermons/1960/george-truett-and-religious-liberty/.

———. "Knowing the Time." Sermon, First Baptist Church of Dallas, January 16, 1955. https://wacriswell.com/sermons/1955/knowing-the-time/.

———. "The Purpose of Prophecy." Sermon, Dallas, January 9, 1972. https://wacriswell.com/sermons/1958/purpose-of-prophecy/.

———. "The Way Back to God." Sermon, First Baptist Church, Dallas, TX. December 31, 1944. https://wacriswell.com/sermons/1944/the-way-back-to-god/.

Cummings, William. "Trump Claims Americans Say 'under God' and 'Merry Christmas' More since He Won." *USA Today*, May 3, 2018. https://www.usatoday.com/story/news/politics/onpolitics/2018/05/03/trump-americans-saying-under-god-more/578069002/.

Cunitz, Edouard, Johann-Wilhelm Baum, and Eduard Wilhelm Eugen Reuss, eds. *Joannis Calvini opera quae supersunt omnia.* Brunsvigae: C. A. Schwetschke, 1863.

Daileader, Philip. *Saint Vincent Ferrer, His World and Life.* New York: Palgrave Macmillan, 2016.

Deane, Jennifer. *A History of Medieval Heresy and Inquisition.* Lanham, Md.: Rowman and Littlefield, 2011.

Docherty, George. *I've Seen the Day.* Grand Rapids: Eerdmans, 1984.

Dochuk, Darren. *From Bible Belt to Sun Belt.* New York: Norton, 2012.

"Donald Trump Campaign Rally in Des Moines, Iowa." C-SPAN, September 13, 2016. Video and transcript. https://www.c-span.org/video/?415184-1%2Fdonald-trump-campaigns-des-moines-iowa.

Early, Joe, Jr. "W. A. Criswell: The Wall of Separation of Church and State and Politics." *Baptist History and Heritage* 43, no. 3 (2008), 82-88.

Edwards, John. *A Compleat History or Survey of All the Dispensations.* London, 1699.

Eisenhower, Dwight D. "The Chance for Peace." Speech, Washington, D.C., April 16, 1953.

———. *Crusade in Europe*. Garden City, N.Y.: Doubleday, 1948.

———. *Papers of Dwight David Eisenhower*. Baltimore: Johns Hopkins University Press, 1970.

Eisenstein, Elizabeth. *The Printing Press as an Agent of Change: Communications and Cultural Transformations in Early Modern Europe*. Cambridge: Cambridge University Press, 1979.

Emmerson, Richard. "The Representation of Antichrist in Hildegard of Bingen's *Scivias*: Image, Word, Commentary, and Visionary Experience." *Gesta* 41, no. 2 (2002), 95-110.

Ephrem the Syrian. *Sancti patris nostri Ephraem Syri Opera omnia*. Translated by Peter Ambarach. Rome: Ex typographia Vaticana, Jo. Mariae Henrici Salvioni, 1737–1743.

———. *Selected Prose Works: Commentary on Genesis, Commentary on Exodus, Homily on Our Lord, Letter to Publius*. Edited by Kathleen McVey. Translated by Edward Mathews Jr. and Joseph Amar. Washington, D.C.: Catholic University of America Press, 1994.

Farrell, James. "Thomas Merton and the Religion of the Bomb." *Religion and American Culture: A Journal of Interpretation* 5, no. 1 (1995): 77–98.

Ferrer, Vincent. "The Report on the Antichrist." In *Historia de la portentosa vida y milagros del Valenciano Apostol de Europa S. Vicente Ferrer, con su misma doctrina reflexionada*. Valencia: En La Oficina de Joseph Estevan Dolz. 1735.

Ford, Gerald. "1976 State of the Union." January 19, 1976. https://www .presidency.ucsb.edu/documents/address-before-joint-session-the -congress-reporting-the-state-the-union.

———. "President Gerald R. Ford's Remarks on Signing a Proclamation Granting Pardon to Richard Nixon." Washington, D.C. September 8, 1974. https://www.fordlibrarymuseum.gov/library/speeches/740060 .asp.

Frady, Marshall. *Billy Graham: A Parable of American Righteousness*. New York: Simon and Schuster, 2006.

Frankopan, Peter. *The First Crusade: The Call from the East*. Cambridge, Mass.: Harvard University Press, 2012.

Gibbs, Nancy, and Michael Duffy. *The Preacher and the Presidents*. New York: Hachette, 2007.

Golgowski, Nina. "Evangelical Christian Billy Graham Stops Calling Mormonism a 'Cult' to Help Romney into the White House." *Daily Mail*, October 18, 2012. https://www.dailymail.co.uk/news/article -2219364/Evangelistic-Association-Reverend-Billy-Graham-stops -calling-Mormonism-cult-meeting-Romney.html.

Goodstein, Laurie. "Billy Graham, 99, Dies; Pastor Filled Stadiums and Counseled Presidents." *New York Times*, February 21, 2018.

Graham, Billy. "America Is in Trouble." Sermon, Minneapolis, 1967. https://billygraham.org/audio/america-is-in-trouble/.

———. "America, Is the Handwriting on the Wall?" Sermon, St. Louis, 1973. https://billygraham.org/audio-cat/sermons/?s=is+the +handwriting+on+the+wall.

———. "America's Greatest Need." Sermon, Minneapolis, 1969. https:// billygraham.org/audio/america-is-the-handwriting-on-the-wall/.

———. "America's Need for Spiritual Awakening." Sermon, Pittsburgh, 1952. https://billygraham.org/audio/americas-need-for-spiritual -awakening/.

———. *Approaching Hoofbeats: The Four Horsemen of the Apocalypse.* Waco, Tex.: Word, 1983.

———. "Can America Survive?" Sermon, Minneapolis, 1968. https:// billygraham.org/audio/can-american-survive/.

———. "Christ Is Coming." Sermon, *Hour of Decision*, 1955. https:// billygraham.org/audio/christ-is-coming/.

———. "The Coming Kingdom." Sermon, Minneapolis, 1970. https:// billygraham.org/audio/the-coming-kingdom/.

———. "The Coming Storm." Sermon, Tempe, Ariz., 1974. https:// billygraham.org/audio/the-coming-storm/.

———. "Communism and Christianity." Sermon, Little Rock, Ark., 1953. https://billygraham.org/audio/communism-and-christianity/.

———. "Dare to Be a Daniel." Sermon, Columbia, S.C., 1987. https:// billygraham.org/audio/dare-to-be-a-daniel/.

———. "The End of the World." Sermon, Montreat, N.C., 1958. https:// billygraham.org/audio/the-end-of-the-world/.

———. "Final Judgment." Sermon, Los Angeles, 1949. https:// billygraham.org/audio/final-judgment/.

———. "The Handwriting on the Wall." Sermon, San Francisco, 1958. https://billygraham.org/audio/the-handwriting-on-the-wall/.

Graham, Billy. Just as I Am. San Francisco: HarperCollins, 1997.

———. "Learning from National Tragedy: A Message from Billy Graham." Sermon, Minneapolis, 1963. https://billygraham.org/audio/how-could-it-happen-in-america/.

———. "The Love of God (Part 1)." Sermon, Baltimore, 2006. https://billygraham.org/audio/the-love-of-god-part-1/.

———. "National Repentance." Sermon, Washington, D.C., 1952. https://billygraham.org/audio/national-repentance/.

———. "Our Nation Must Repent." Sermon, *Hour of Decision*, 1957. https://billygraham.org/audio/our-nation-must-repent/.

———. "Preparation for Armageddon." Sermon, Minneapolis, 1967. https://billygraham.org/audio/preparation-for-armageddon/.

———. "Prepare to Meet Thy God." Sermon, Washington, D.C., 1952. https://billygraham.org/audio/prepare-to-meet-thy-god/.

———. "Mr. President." Sermon, St. Louis, 1953. https://billygraham.org/audio/mr-president/.

———. "Reverend Billy Graham's Reaction following the Assassination of President John F. Kennedy." Speech, Dallas, November 1963. https://www.youtube.com/watch?v=PsjlnHHZYjk.

———. "Request for Prayer for Washington." Sermon, Greensboro, N.C., 1951. https://billygraham.org/audio/request-for-prayer-for-washington/.

———. "The Rise of the AntiChrist." Sermon, *Hour of Decision*, 1972. https://billygraham.org/audio/the-rise-of-the-antichrist/.

———. "The Second Coming of Christ." Sermon, Los Angeles, 1949. https://billygraham.org/audio/the-second-coming-of-christ/.

———. "Shadows of the Great Antichrist." Sermon, Minneapolis, 1967. https://billygraham.org/audio/shadows-of-the-great-antichrist/.

———. *Storm Warning*. Dallas: Word, 1992. 2nd ed., Nashville: Thomas Nelson, 2011.

———. "The Supreme Court Ruling on Prayer." Sermon, Minneapolis, 1962. https://billygraham.org/audio/the-supreme-court-ruling-on-prayer/.

———. "Warnings to America." Sermon, SS *United States*, 1954. https://billygraham.org/audio/warnings-to-america/.

———. "Ways America May Continue to Prosper." Sermon, New Orleans, 1954. https://billygraham.org/audio/ways-america-may-continue-to-prosper/.

———. "When Will the End of the World Come?" Sermon, Bristol, England, 1984. https://billygraham.org/audio/when-will-the-end-of-the-world-come-2/.

———. "Why God Allows Communism to Flourish." Sermon, Los Angeles, 1949. https://billygraham.org/audio/why-god-allows-communism-to -flourish/.

———. *World Aflame*. New York: Doubleday, 1965.

Graham, Ruth. "New Ad from Anti-Trump Christian Group Vote Common Good Juxtaposes a 1973 Billy Graham Sermon with Trump Clips, Set to Mozart's Requiem." Twitter, September 22, 2020. https:// twitter.com/publicroad/status/1308480576895287298?s=20.

Grant, Tobin, "Why 1940s America Wasn't as Religious as You Think—the Rise and Fall of American Religion." *Religion News Service*, December 11, 2014. https://religionnews.com/2014/12/11/ 1940s-america-wasnt-religious-think-rise-fall-american-religion/.

Graves, Robert. *The Greek Myths: The Complete and Definitive Edition*. London: Penguin, 2017.

Grossman, Cathy Lynn. "Billy Graham, America's Pastor, Has Died." *USA Today*, February 21, 2018.

Helmore, Edward. "'How Is This Not Inciting Violence?': Gun Shop Billboard Targets the 'Squad.'" *Guardian*, August 1, 2019.

Henry, Patrick. "'And I Don't Care What It Is': The Tradition-History of a Civil Religion Proof-Text." *Journal of the American Academy of Religion* 49, no. 1 (1981): 35–49.

Hidal, Sten, and Knud Jeppesen. "Apocalypse, Persecution and Exegesis: Hippolytus and Theodoret of Cyrrhus on the Book of Daniel." In *In the Last Days: On Jewish and Christian Apocalyptic and Its Period*, edited by Knud Jeppesen, Kirsten Nielsen, and Bent Rosendal, 49–53. Aarhus, Denmark: Aarhus University Press, 1994.

Irénée de Lyon. *Contre les hérésies. Livre IV. Édition critique d'après les versions arménienne et latine 1–2*. Éd. Bertrand Hemmerdinger, Louis Doutreleau, Charles Mercier. Sources chrétiennes 100. Paris: Cerf, 1965.

Jenkins, Jack. "Ahead of Trump Bible Photo Op, Police Forcibly Expel Priest from St. John's Church near White House." *Religion News Service*, June 3, 2020. https://religionnews.com/2020/06/02/ahead -of-trump-bible-photo-op-police-forcibly-expel-priest-from-st -johns-church-near-white-house/?fbclid=IwAR3XjhVL9SgzXchn -MjzfrSEi1dPIkxpx7My3MVMSC0FTUCy0UPuDCYnuzw.

Jerome. S. *Hieronymi Presbyteri Opera. Pars I: Opera Exegetica, 6; Commentarii in Prophetas Minores*. Edited by M. Adriaen. Corpus Christianorum Series Latina 76. Turnhout: Brepols, 1969.

Johnson, Jenna, and Abigail Hauslohner. "'I Think Islam Hates Us': A Timeline of Trump's Comments about Islam and Muslims." *Washington Post,* May 20, 2017. https://www.washingtonpost.com/news/post-politics/wp/2017/05/20/i-think-islam-hates-us-a-timeline-of-trumps-comments-about-islam-and-muslims/.

Johnson, Lyndon Baines. "President Johnson's Special Message to the Congress: The American Promise." March 15, 1965. Video and transcript. LBJ Presidential Library. http://www.lbjlibrary.org/lyndon-baines-johnson/speeches-films/president-johnsons-special-message-to-the-congress-the-american-promise.

Klaas, Brian. "A Short History of President Trump's Anti-Muslim Bigotry." *Washington Post,* March 15, 2019. https://www.washingtonpost.com/opinions/2019/03/15/short-history-president-trumps-anti-muslim-bigotry/.

Knorr, N. H. "Religion Void of Principle." *Awake!* October 22, 1946.

Koerner, Joseph. *The Reformation of the Image.* Chicago: University of Chicago Press, 2004.

Krey, Philip. Introduction to *Nicholas of Lyra: The Senses of Scripture,* edited by Philip Krey and Lesley Smith, 1–18. Leiden: Brill, 2000.

———. "The Law and the Jews in Nicholas of Lyra's Romans Commentary of 1329." In *Nicholas of Lyra: The Senses of Scripture,* edited by Philip Krey and Lesley Smith, 251–66. Leiden: Brill, 2000.

Kruse, Kevin. *One Nation under God: How Corporate America Invented Christian America.* New York: Basic Books, 2015.

Lacey, Marc. "Clinton Ranks in the Middle, But Falls Last On Morality." *New York Times,* February 21, 2000. https://www.nytimes.com/2000/02/21/us/clinton-ranks-in-the-middle-but-falls-last-on-morality.html.

LeBlanc, Paul. "Bishop at DC Church Outraged by Trump Visit: 'I Just Can't Believe What My Eyes Have Seen.'" *CNN,* June 2, 2020. https://www.cnn.com/2020/06/01/politics/cnntv-bishop-trump-photo-op/index.html.

Lewis, Donald M. *The Origins of Christian Zionism: Lord Shaftesbury and Evangelical Support for a Jewish Homeland.* Cambridge: Cambridge University Press, 2010.

Lord Roy, Ralph. *Apostles of Discord.* Boston: Beacon, 1953.

Luther, Martin. *D. Martin Luther's Werke: Kritische Gesamtausgabe (Weimarer Ausgabe).* Weimar: H. Böhlaus Nachfolger, 1883.

———. *Luther's Works.* Edited by Jaroslav Pelikan, Hilton C. Oswald, Helmut T. Lehmann, Christopher Boyd Brown, Benjamin T. G.

Mayes, and James Langebartels. American ed. 55 vols. Saint Louis: Concordia; Philadelphia: Fortress, 1955–1986.

Martin, William. *A Prophet with Honor: The Billy Graham Story*. Grand Rapids: Zondervan, 2018.

Marty, Martin. *Modern American Religion*. Vol. 3, *Under God, Indivisible, 1941–1960*. Chicago: University of Chicago Press, 1996.

McCammon, Sarah. "What Does Trump's Promise of a Nation 'under One God' Really Mean?" *NPR*, September 18, 2016. https://www.npr.org/2016/09/18/494367803/what-does-trumps-promise-of-a-nation-under-one-god-really-mean.

McGinn, Bernard. *Visions of the End*. New York: Columbia University Press, 1998.

Merritt, Jonathan. "Billy Graham, the Last Nonpartisan Evangelical?" *New York Times*, February 21, 2018.

Mills, James. "The Serious Implications of a 1971 Conversation with Ronald Reagan." *San Diego Magazine*, August 1985.

National Secular Society. "George Bush on Atheists as Citizens or Patriots." February 6, 2004. https://www.secularism.org.uk/33034.html.

Newport, Frank. "Five Key Findings on Religion in the U.S." *Gallup*, December 23, 2016. https://news.gallup.com/poll/200186/five-key-findings-religion.aspx.

Nicholas of Lyra. "Daniel." In *Bibliorum Sacrorum cum Glossa Ordinaria*, vol. 4, 1489–693. Venice, 1603.

Nixon, Richard. *The Memoirs of Richard Nixon*. New York: Grosset and Dunlap, 1978.

Noll, Mark. *A History of Christianity in the United States and Canada*. Grand Rapids: Eerdmans, 1992.

Oakman, Charles. "Abraham Lincoln: Extension of Remarks of Hon. Charles G. Oakman." *Congressional Record*, vol. 100, session 2, February 12, 1954.

Obama, Barack. "Address to Congress on the American Jobs Act." September 8, 2011. Video and transcript. Miller Center, University of Virginia. https://millercenter.org/the-presidency/presidential-speeches/september-8-2011-address-congress-american-jobs-act.

———. "Remarks on the Death of Osama bin Laden." May 1, 2011. Video and transcript. Miller Center, University of Virginia. https://millercenter.org/the-presidency/presidential-speeches/may-1-2011-remarks-death-osama-bin-laden.

Ockenga, Harold. "The Ethiopian Situation, or The Meaning of the Present World Crisis." Sermon, Point Breeze Presbyterian Church, Boston, 1935.

———. "God Save America." Sermon, Park Street Church, Boston, September 1939.

Oecolampadius, Johann. *Commentariorum Ioannis Oecolampadii in Danielem prophetam libri duo, abstrusiore tum Hebraeorum tum Graecorum scriptorum doctrina referti.* Genevae: [Ioannis Crispini], 1553.

Ohlheiser, Abby. "Why President Obama Didn't Say 'under God' while Reading the Gettysburg Address." *Yahoo! News*, November 19, 2013. https://news.yahoo.com/why-president-obama-didnt-under-god-while-reading-191035734.html.

Orin, Deborah. "Bush: One Nation, under God." *New York Post*, July 5, 2002. https://nypost.com/2002/07/05/bush-one-nation-under-god/.

Parker, Ashley. "In Romney's Hands, Pledge of Allegiance Is Framework for Criticism." *New York Times*, September 8, 2012.

Pengelly, Martin. "Trump Spreads False Claim Democrats Dropped God from Pledge of Allegiance." *Guardian*, August 22, 2020. https://www.theguardian.com/us-news/2020/aug/22/donald-trump-democrats-god-pledge.

Pitkin, Barbara. "Prophecy and History in Calvin's Lectures on Daniel." In *Die Geschichte der Daniel-Auslegung in Judentum, Christentum und Islam*, edited by Katharina Bracht et al., 323–48. Berlin: De Gruyter, 2007.

"President Donald J. Trump Stands Up for Religious Freedom in the United States." May 3, 2018. WhiteHouse.gov. https://trumpwhitehouse.archives.gov/briefings-statements/president-donald-j-trump-stands-religious-freedom-united-states/.

"President Hails Revised Pledge." *New York Times*, June 15, 1954.

Reagan, Ronald. "Evil Empire." March 8, 1983. https://millercenter.org/the-presidency/presidential-speeches/march-8-1983-evil-empire-speech.

———. "Farewell Address at the Republican National Convention." August 15, 1988. https://millercenter.org/the-presidency/presidential-speeches/august-15-1988-farewell-address-republican-national-convention.

———. "Inaugural Address, January 20, 1981." In *Public Papers of the Presidents: Ronald Reagan 1981.* Washington, D.C.: United States Government Printing Office, 1982.

———. *The Reagan Diaries.* Edited by Douglas Brinkley. New York: Harper Collins, 2007.

———. "Remarks at an Ecumenical Prayer Breakfast in Dallas, Texas." Speech, Dallas, August 23, 1984. https://www.reaganfoundation.org/media/128825/dallas.pdf.

———. "Second Inaugural Address." January 21, 1985. https://millercenter.org/the-presidency/presidential-speeches/january-21-1985-second-inaugural-address.

———. "State of the Union Address." January 26, 1982. https://nebrwesleyan-my.sharepoint.com/:x:/g/personal/rlester_nebrwesleyan_edu/EcFWcu-GfaVHpmgBkWtB5YUB5RbxwG7fGOF0HKWFBrjwSA?e=i7kQye.

———. "State of the Union Address." January 25, 1983. https://millercenter.org/the-presidency/presidential-speeches/january-25-1983-state-union-address.

———. "State of the Union." February 6, 1985. https://millercenter.org/the-presidency/presidential-speeches/february-6-1985-state-union-address.

———. "State of the Union." February 4, 1986. https://millercenter.org/the-presidency/presidential-speeches/february-4-1986-state-union-address.

———. "A Time for Choosing." In *The U.S. Constitution: A Reader*, edited by Hillsdale College Politics Faculty, 773–84. Hillsdale, Mich.: Hillsdale College Press, 2012.

———. "1980 Republican National Convention Acceptance Speech." July 17, 1980. https://millercenter.org/the-presidency/presidential-speeches/july-17-1980-republican-national-convention.

———. "Republican National Convention Acceptance Speech." August 23, 1984. https://millercenter.org/the-presidency/presidential-speeches/august-23-1984-republican-national-convention.

Reeves, Marjorie. *Joachim of Fiore and the Prophetic Future*. Cheltenham, UK: Sutton, 1999.

Reid, W. Stanford. "The Four Monarchies of Daniel in Reformation Historiography." *Historical Reflections / Réflexions Historiques* 8, no. 1 (1981): 115–23.

Reitman, Alan. Memorandum to Washington office. May 24, 1954, box 1, ACLU.

Rice, John R. "Is Mussolini the Anti-Christ?" *Sword of the Lord* 1, no. 9 (1935): 1 and 4.

Riley, William Bell. "Coming Armageddon." Sermon, First Baptist Church Minneapolis, 1940. https://cdm16120.contentdm.oclc.org/digital/collection/riley/id/3694/rec/4.

———. "The Kingdom of God—Its Location." *The Northwestern Pilot*, July 1954, 11–16.

Roberts, Alexander, and James Donaldson, eds. *Apostolic Fathers, Justin Martyr, Irenaeus*. Vol. 1 of *Ante-Nicene Fathers*. New York: Charles Scribner's Sons, 1903.

Rosell, Garth. *The Surprising Work of God: Harold John Ockenga, Billy Graham, and the Rebirth of Evangelicalism*. Grand Rapids: Baker, 2008.

Runciman, Steven. *A History of the Crusades*. Vol. 2, *The Kingdom of Jerusalem*. New York: Cambridge University Press, 1995.

Ryrie, Charles C. *Dispensationalism*. Chicago: Moody, 1995.

Scofield, Cyrus I. Introduction to *The Scofield Reference Bible*. Edited and annotated by Cyrus I. Scofield. New York: Oxford University Press, 1917.

———. *Rightly Dividing the Word of Truth*. 1888. http://biblecentre.org/content.php?mode=7&item=777.

Selnecker, Nikolaus. *Der Prophet Daniel, und die Offenbarung Johannis*. Germany: Berwalt, 1567.

Shabecoff, Philip. "Presidency Is Found Weaker under Ford." *New York Times*, March 28, 1976.

Shelton, W. Brian. *Martyrdom from Exegesis in Hippolytus: An Early Church Presbyter's Commentary on Daniel*. Eugene, Ore.: Wipf and Stock, 2008.

Siacon, Aleanna. "Rep. Rashida Tlaib Slams North Carolina Gun Billboard for 'Inciting Violence.'" *Asheville Citizen-Times*, July 31, 2019.

Smith, Gary Scott. *Religion in the Oval Office*. New York: Oxford University Press, 2015.

Sutton, Matthew Avery. *American Apocalypse: A History of Modern Evangelicalism*. Cambridge, Mass.: Belknap Press of Harvard University Press, 2014.

Timmerman, Daniel. "The World Always Perishes, the Church Will Last Forever: Church and Eschatology in Bullinger's Sermons on the Book of Daniel (1565)." *Zwingliana* 36 (2009): 85–101.

Truett, George. "Baptists and Religious Liberty." Sermon, Washington, D.C., 1920. http://www.reformedreader.org/baptistsandreligiousliberty.htm.

Trump, Donald J. "Remarks by President Trump at the National Day of Prayer." May 3, 2018. WhiteHouse.gov. https://trumpwhitehouse.archives.gov/briefings-statements/remarks-president-trump-national-day-prayer/.

————. "Speech at the Veterans of Foreign Wars National Convention." July 24, 2018. Video and transcript. Miller Center, University of Virginia. https://millercenter.org/the-presidency/presidential-speeches/july-24-2018-speech-veterans-foreign-wars-national-convention.

————. "State of the Union Address." February 5, 2019. Video and transcript. Miller Center, University of Virginia. https://millercenter.org/the-presidency/presidential-speeches/february-5-2019-state-union-address.

————. "We Believe that Every American Should Stand for the National Anthem, and We Proudly Pledge Allegiance to One NATION UNDER GOD!" Twitter, December 9, 2017. https://twitter.com/realdonaldtrump/status/939375570919612416?lang=en.

Truman, Harry S. "Inaugural Address." Washington, D.C. January 20, 1949. https://avalon.law.yale.edu/20th_century/truman.asp.

"Trump to Anthem Protesters: 'Get That Son of a B—— Off the Field.'" NBC Sports, September 22, 2017. https://www.nbcsports.com/bayarea/49ers/trump-anthem-protesters-get-son-b-field.

Van Liere, Frans. "The Literal Sense of the Books of Samuel and Kings: From Andrew of St. Victor to Nicholas of Lyra." In *Nicholas of Lyra: The Senses of Scripture*, edited by Philip Krey and Lesley Smith, 59–82 Leiden: Brill, 2000.

Vogel, Winfried. "The Eschatological Theology of Martin Luther—Part II: Luther's Exposition of Daniel and Revelation." *Andrews University Seminary Studies* 25, no. 2 (1987): 183–99.

Wacker, Grant. *America's Pastor*. Cambridge, Mass.: Harvard University Press, 2014.

Wakefield, Walter L., and Austin P. Evans. *Heresies of the High Middle Ages*. New York: Columbia University Press, 1991.

"'We Are Better Off Today,' Says George H. W. Bush." NBC News, September 1, 2004. http://www.nbcnews.com/id/5889684/ns/msnbc-imus_on_msnbc/t/we-are-better-today-says-george-h-w-bush/#.XpY5tchKhz1.

Wehner, Peter. "Are Trump's Critics Demonically Possessed?" *Atlantic*, November 25, 2019. https://www.theatlantic.com/ideas/archive/2019/11/to-trumps-evangelicals-everyone-else-is-a-sinner/602569/.

INDEX